the GREAT PATRIOT

BUY-cott Book:

The Great Conservative Companies to BUY From!

The Winning Game Plan to DEFUND Leftist
Woke Companies and FUND Conservative,
Patriotic & Christian Companies!

WAYNE ALLYN ROOT
& NICKY BILLOU

CONTENTS

Section 1: What Patriots Believe

Section 2: Why We Believe Elections Are Being Stolen

Section 3: We Believe the Covid Vaccine is Dangerous and Deadly. It Has to be Stopped. And the People Who Pushed It Must Be Held Accountable

Section 4: The Global Fight For Freedom

Section 5: The List

"The urge to save humanity is almost always a false front for the urge to rule."

H.L. Mencken

FOREWORD

I believe that this is *the single most important book to place in the hands of our citizens, in order to preserve our nation and our way of life.*

That is a bold statement! And my goal here is to explain how and why this is so.

The "Deconstruction" of America

The "woke" Marxists who are hell-bent on destroying our nation have repeatedly and openly declared their intention to "deconstruct" everything that we love. Look online for "deconstructing the family" (45,500,000 results on Google) or "deconstructing American history" (7,200,000 results) or "deconstructing religion" (6,410,000 results) and you will find vast numbers of "academic" works declaring such objectives.

But what does "deconstruct" actually mean? It means "destroy." To break something down to its component parts. To atomize. To annihilate.

In private, among themselves, the woke folk often exhort each other to, "Burn it to the ground."

Motivated by hate, envy, and spite, their goal is to destroy everything we love, and rebuild it from the ground up. With, of course, themselves in power.

This is the very definition of evil. Destructive, hateful, envious, spiteful evil.

The Opposite of Evil

Now, let me pose a simple question: "What is the opposite of evil?" No. The opposite of evil is not good. The opposite of evil is *love.*

Evil is the absence of love, just as darkness is the absence of light. And we can defeat evil with love.

Love for our families, our nation, and our God. These are the weapons that we can use to fight an evil that is threatening and actively destroying everything that we love.

And this book (along with its worthy predecessor, ***The Great Patriot Protest & Boycott Book***) is *the essential resource* to empower us, to equip us and guide us, in order to focus "our lives, our fortunes, and our sacred honor" toward the vital endeavor of protecting what we love.

Our enemy's openly avowed objective is to destroy. Our goal is to preserve, protect, and conserve all that is good and worthy. (Thus the term "conservative.")

We win by focusing our every penny (our cents and our good sense), toward upholding worthy, patriotic, and virtuous businesses.

Get Woke, Go Broke... On Steroids!

You've probably heard the phrase: "Get woke, go broke." And we can give you many great examples. But the woke folk don't care if they destroy a company or bankrupt an industry. They truly want to destroy – i.e. "deconstruct" – not just our businesses, but our entire nation! The trail of busted businesses, broken dreams, and destroyed lives that they leave behind them are "virtue signals" of their faith, the glorious "stigmata" of their religion.

What we must understand is that this Marxist, socialist, woke belief *is their religion.* (Like a religion, it has to be taken on faith, it has never been proven to work.) This is their religion, and they as zealous and fanatical as any suicide bomber.

If "get woke, go broke" hasn't defeated them yet, then what is our strategy? Well, Ronald Reagan defeated the Soviet Union by "doubling down" on the Cold War. Like all such Marxist socialist states, the

USSR was doomed to ultimate failure and collapse. But the question was: "How much more harm will they do? How many more millions will they exterminate? Before this hideous evil beast finally dies?"

The answer for President Reagan was simple: keep doing the honorable, virtuous, right thing. Except, *even more so!*

And the answer for us is just as simple: "Get woke, go broke, *on steroids!*" Kick in the afterburners!

Again: we win by focusing our every penny (our cents and our good sense), toward upholding worthy, patriotic, and virtuous businesses. Every single dollar you spend is a soldier in this battle. Will your "troops" fight for what you love, or will you aid and abet the treacherous evil that wants to "deconstruct" our families, our faith, and our nation?

I implore you. I beseech you! As we love our nation. As we love our families, and our God: make this book the "gameplan" for virtuous victory. Use your love to defeat evil! Apply this book (and its predecessor, **The Great Patriot Protest & Boycott Book**) to every aspect of your life! Buy a copy for all your friends. Get a copy for every family member. Bring it to your house of worship and encourage others to join you in this epic battle against the forces of evil!

Remember, the opposite of evil is love. Will you join us in the battle to protect everything that you love?

Lt. Col. Dave Grossman, USA (ret.)
www.GrossmanOnTruth.com
Author of On Killing, On Combat, On Hunting, On Spiritual Combat, Assassination Generation, **and** *The Sheepdogs: Meet Our Nation's Warriors* **children's book.**

INTRODUCTION

We are living in perilous times. The forces of darkness have successfully marched through many of the great institutions of American life and are in the process of doing their damnedest to extinguish freedom in America. Until recently, they had not turned their sights on corporate America. But in the past ten years, the Left has gone on offense against big business, threatening them with cancellation unless they toed the woke line.

Big business has never been a bastion of courage. They have always followed the doctrine of popular culture (and never led it). The threat of cancellation has forced thousands of the biggest businesses in America to embrace "wok-ism" as a way of inoculating themselves against the wrath of the Left. Most of the executives who run these companies don't really care about woke or liberal ideology, but they are frightened to death of losing their jobs or being canceled, so they toe the line. They hire and promote woke employees. They give lip service to woke causes and sometimes even send millions of dollars to help fund them. They get supported by normal, regular patriotic Americans (like you and me) who patronize their businesses, and then turn around, take our money and spit in the face of their customers and their values.

More ominously, the problem is that these companies' support for woke causes is destroying everything that has made America great. Support for BLM has caused that organization to feel emboldened and to lead riots that have destroyed billions in property and led to the dozens of deaths. Inserting mature sexual themes in Disney's programming for 5- to 8-year-olds is sexualizing little children, grooming them for molestation and exploitation, and leading to terrible decisions to change their gender at an age too young to make life-altering decisions. Anyone who speaks out against this terrible attack on America and our religious values is attacked by the woke mob, who then pushes hard to have them canceled.

This is the tactic of the schoolyard bully. First, hit someone, then intimidate them (and others) into compliance.

But like all bullies, all that needs to happen to scare off the woke bullies is for good, decent folks to stand up to them and give them a metaphorical punch in the nose. You've got to hit back, otherwise, the bully will keep hitting you and scaring all your friends into compliance with their arrogant and unreasonable demands.

In our last book, **The Great Patriot Protest & Boycott Book,** we outlined how freedom-loving Americans (like you) can fight back against the cancel culture bullies by going on offense against the woke companies. In this book, we made a list of 116 woke American corporations, we published their names, their CEOs' names, Board of Directors, corporate addresses, email addresses, and social media handles. We encouraged our readers to vote with their dollars and take their business away from these dangerous woke companies. We also encouraged them to respectfully, but firmly, write to the CEOs of the companies, and tell them that they are taking their business elsewhere, and why.

We want 150 million Americans to stop doing business with woke corporations. The average American spends $30,000 a year with these woke companies. That's $4.5 trillion dollars! Imagine if we can divert even a portion of those trillions of dollars in the next 12 months? That would force these woke companies to sit up and take notice of the concerns of patriotic Americans (aka, their customer base).

We need to make these CEOs more afraid of offending us, their customers, than of offending the woke mob, who are not their customers.

Taking away trillions of dollars in revenue would have a devastating effect on hundreds of these woke companies. Their shareholders would demand that they drop the woke politics and stick to business. CEO and board members would lose their jobs for non-performance, forcing many woke companies to drop their adherence to woke liberal agendas or go bankrupt.

The urgency of uniting Americans in divesting themselves from the products and services offered by these woke companies has never been greater. The leaked internal video from Disney, where the President of one of their divisions BRAGGED about inserting mature LGBTQ themes into programming for 5-to-8-year-old kids, horrified all sane Americans. Little kids should not be exposed to sexual themes of any kind, as this could lead to them being exploited and molested. The impact of this on them is catastrophic. Children who have been molested or sexualized when they are very young often develop major issues surrounding self-esteem, the ability to successfully form healthy relationships, performance in school, truancy, and the susceptibility to become exploiters and abusers of children themselves. It is IMPERATIVE that we push back against this, hard.

A report by the American Psychological Association (APA) released in 2007 provided evidence that "the proliferation of sexualized images of girls and young women in advertising, merchandising, and media is harmful to girls' self-image and healthy development."

"The APA Task Force on the Sexualization of Girls" examined published research on the content and effects of virtually every form of media, including television, music videos, music lyrics, magazines, movies, video games and the Internet. They also examined recent advertising campaigns and merchandising of products aimed toward girls.

"Sexualization" was defined by the task force as "occurring when a person's values come only from her/his sexual appeal or behavior to the exclusion of other characteristics, and when a person is sexually objectified, e.g., made into a thing for another's sexual use."

A member of the Task Force, Dr. Sharon Lamb, a Clinical Psychologist and Professor of Psychology at Saint Michael's College, is the co-author with Lyn Mikel Brown of the book "**Packaging Girlhood: Rescuing Our Daughters from Marketers' Schemes**" (St. Martin's Press, 2006). She has also written on "normal" sexual development in girls and on how therapists can treat sexual issues as they arise in therapeutic encounters with children and teens. Her research on girls' development, teenagers and sex, and abuse and victimization were a foundation for the Task Force's report.

Dr. Eileen Zurbriggen, an Associate Professor at the University of California Santa Cruz, and the Chair of the APA Task Force, stated, "As a society, we need to replace all these sexualized images with ones showing girls in positive settings—ones that show the uniqueness and competence of girls. The goal should be to deliver messages to all adolescents—boys and girls—that lead to healthy sexual development."

On his website www.drdennycoates.com, Dr. Denny Coates features an article by Dr. Elizabeth McDade-Montez, a Senior Research Associate at www.etr.org (Education, Training, and Research), who has studied the influence of media on children and adolescents. She says that "when it comes to sex education, parents need to learn more about how our culture sexualizes their kids."

"If you have growing children, you probably make a considerable effort to protect them from troublesome or harmful media content. Whether you watch on TV, YouTube, Netflix, or some other platform, chances are you search out media geared towards your children's age and developmental level."

"I recently conducted an analysis of popular children's television shows (aimed at ages 6 —11) that suggests it may be quite difficult to find shows without content that features sexualization. In fact, I would go so far as to call my findings disturbing."

"Sexualization was present in every episode! Yes, every one of the 30 episodes representing the most popular shows included examples of sexualization. Furthermore, instances of sexualization were frequent. There were an average of 24 instances of sexualization per episode."

"The most common forms of sexualization included self-sexualizing behaviors, such as wearing revealing clothing or heavy makeup, but there were also instances of more aggressive forms of sexualization, including sexual harassment and unwanted sexual touching."

Why does this matter?

"Media content affects a variety of health behaviors in children, including sexual activity, aggression, and mental health."

"For example, exposure to music with degrading, sexualized lyrics is associated with the early experience of sexual intercourse. Watching

X-rated movies is associated with a greater likelihood of dating violence. Exposure to sexualized ideas has been linked to low self-esteem, negative mood and symptoms of depression in adolescent(s)."

Someone ought to tell Disney that.

Disney has now become the poster child for woke corporate America. The company, led by ex-CEO Bob Chapek, decided to publicly oppose Florida's thoughtful and nuanced anti-grooming bill, which prohibits sexualizing kids aged 5-8 (kindergarteners through third grade) with sexual content. Disney caved to its extreme, woke employees, and falsely accused Governor Ron DeSantis of crafting an "anti LGBTQ bill." They accelerated their sick, twisted internal policy of mature LGBTQ themes in their popular children's programming (!!!!&^*^&P*!!!#***). Our little kids are now being regularly indoctrinated with adult sexual themes. The new Disney CEO Bob Iger seems to be backing off. Yet, in the same breath, he promises LGBTQ themes inside Disney shows.

This is INSANE! Any honest psychologist would tell you that sexualizing little kids and programming their minds with the normalization of sex at a young age is bad for their development, bad for the future of our society, and just plain wrong.

This agenda by Disney had both of us (coauthors Wayne and Nicky) up in arms, and we decided to go on offense and lead the charge against Disney with our last book. Our readers responded magnificently! They have written letters to the CEO, tagged Disney and its CEO on social media with respectful yet firm posts expressing their displeasure, and, most importantly, voted with their dollars and canceled trips to Disney's many theme parks and their subscriptions to the Disney+ streaming service. We also encouraged our fans and supporters to sell off any Disney stock in their retirement accounts. Disney stock plummeted. Disney has lost billions in stock value.

The state of Florida, led by its great Governor, Ron DeSantis, also pushed back hard against Disney. DeSantis and the Republican-led state legislature just passed a law ending 55 years of special tax status for Disney in the state of Florida. Disney has been shocked into silence, and its media allies are bemoaning its fate. Leftists and woke ideologues all over the nation are whining like spoiled brats who finally have to face the consequences of their bad behavior. This is delicious *Schadenfreude* (the German word for taking delight in the misfortune visited upon your enemies).

Twitter is another company that had strayed from its original free speech mission to become a bought and paid-for arm of the woke left and the Democrat Party. It had been silencing conservative voices, beginning with Alex Jones and culminating with the sitting President of the United States, Donald J. Trump, and yours truly (Wayne Allyn Root). Nicky (the co-author of this book) was so disgusted by Twitter's behavior that he canceled his account. The founder of Twitter, Jack Dorsey, himself no friend to free speech, was forced out and replaced by Parag Agarwal, who took his Orwellian, anti-conservative bigotry to new lows, censoring mainstream voices like Project Veritas, Wayne Allyn Root, Libs of TikTok, and many others.

This got the attention of Elon Musk, who decided to do something about it. Musk bought up 9.2% of the company and was offered a board seat, but no real voice in transforming the company into a free speech-friendly place. So, he then came forward with a $43 billion takeover offer. Liberal heads exploded everywhere. And now, Twitter has joined the ranks of non-woke companies.

The emails Musk is now releasing prove a conspiracy by the FBI, the Biden administration and Twitter (along with other social media companies) to rig and steal the 2020 election—by silencing and censoring conservative influencers, releasing propaganda disguised as "news," and censoring/suppressing any news beneficial to President Trump and damaging to candidate Joe Biden. Yes, folks, the 2020 election was, in fact, rigged and stolen. Thank you, Elon Musk, for releasing the truth.

Exxon just announced that it will not allow pro-LGBTQ and BLM flags to be flown outside of its headquarters. Media talking heads and woke leftists are losing their minds over this one. But Exxon's leadership is standing firm, stating that they are not in the business of taking political sides, and will stick to business.

Netflix, whom last year came out with a show called *"Cuties"* that sexualized 11 and 12-year-old girls, just came out with a show called

"He's Expecting" about a man who is pregnant with a child. Unlike previous shows where men were pregnant, this one is not a comedy and is a cave by Netflix to the 0.1% of its subscribers that are radical LGBTQ extremists. These, and other Netflix actions that have focused on promoting a woke ideology, have caused a mass exodus of customers. Subscribers have been deserting Netflix in droves, and its stock price plummeted by over 30% in less than a week. (Of course, the great news is Disney's stock decline is far greater than that.)

All this, plus the inclusion of Netflix in our Boycott list, prompted Netflix to send out a "culture memo" in response to some woke employees being offended, specifically at a Dave Chappelle comedy special where the employees claimed he made "transphobic" comments. The Netflix memo suggests that employees who have a problem with its programming decisions should consider finding another job, as any attempts to silence "artistic expression" will not be entertained, nor will it "censor specific artists or voices" even if an employee considers it "harmful." "If you'd find it hard to support our content breadth, Netflix may not be the best place for you," said the memo.

The ultra-woke Bed, Bath and Beyond corporation was another company included on our boycott list. They famously dropped patriot CEO Mike Lindell's MyPillow from the suppliers whose brands they carried, and patriots responded by not shopping there anymore. They are now on the verge of declaring bankruptcy.

Ultra-woke Victoria's Secret CEO Amy Hauk resigned after less than a year on the job. She is the "genius" who took the company woke by having it hire plus-size models and its first male model and expand the size of its garments. That wrecked a brand that had been built to cater to those who aspire to a traditional ideal of beauty and sexiness. Those customers abandoned it in droves.

We are both encouraged and heartened by the American people's response to Disney, Twitter, Target, Netflix, Bed, Bath & Beyond, Victoria's Secret and other woke companies. It's important that we keep up the pressure and take away our business from Disney and other companies like it. Voting with our dollars is the best way to punish these miscreants and let them know we mean business.

But it's not nearly enough. We can't just punish Disney (and others like them) for their woke behavior and their assault on our values (and especially our children). We also need to find companies that reflect our values, are horrified by the exploitation and grooming of children, and offer great quality products and services that satisfy our needs while supporting a pro-America, pro-Judeo-Christian values, pro-capitalism agenda.

We need to do business with them instead of those that support the destruction of America, American exceptionalism and family values.

This book is all about helping 80+ million Trump warriors (although we both suspect that number has climbed considerably since the 2020 election and the disaster that is the Biden Administration) to create our own conservative business ecosystem.

We need to stop doing business with the woke companies and start doing business with the patriotic ones.

In our last book, we put together a list of 116 woke companies to boycott. We feel like we made a difference. Ask Disney.

In this book, we have put together a list of 123 patriotic companies <u>to buy from</u>.

We have taken our time to put this list together, and it includes companies that are run by patriots that want to uphold America, American exceptionalism, American values, Judeo-Christian values, patriotism and capitalism in their businesses and product offerings.

We will do a short write-up for each company, and we will highlight the products and services that they offer, and encourage you to contact them, offer expressions of support via email and social media posts, and to buy their products and services and encourage your friends, family and business associates (your sphere of influence) to do the same.

Complaining about these woke companies isn't enough. We all must show leadership and support conservative and patriotic companies that provide viable alternatives to the woke liberal companies destroying our country and values. Cancel culture can cut both ways. We can DEFUND the weak, feckless, cowardly companies that are embracing woke-ism, and at the same time, FUND the companies that are embracing patriotism and American exceptionalism.

Conservatives have a real opportunity to vote with our wallets! Let's make every dollar count and get right to it!

By the way, we are putting together a Designation, the "Free Corp™", which has six categories for determining where a company stands on values that matter to its patriotic customer base. We call this the "Freedom Scale."

These are:

1. Political Involvement—Do they stick to business, or are they virtue signalling and supporting leftist causes? Scoring is on a 1 to 5 Scale, 1 being they are virtue signalling and cravenly caving to the woke mob, and 5 is that they refuse to be bullied and tell the woke mob to go to hell.
2. Political donations—To which political candidates and causes do they donate? Do they donate to woke, liberal and Marxist organizations and candidates—such as BLM, Media Matters, the ACLU, the Democrat Party, and Planned Parenthood—or to patriotic and conservative ones—the GOP, RNC, MAGA, NRA, National Right to Life, Project Veritas, etc.? Scoring is on a 1 to 5 Scale, 1 is they give exclusively to woke causes and 5 is they give exclusively to patriot ones.
3. Workplace culture—Is their workplace culture one that embraces freedom or is it poisoned by political correctness? Do they promote freedom and free expression at work, or are some

opinions more equal than others? Do they pressure their employees to toe the woke line: pro-child grooming, pro-denying biology, pro-socialism and Marxism, pro-shutting down free speech...versus pro-family, pro-God, pro-biology, pro-free speech, pro-capitalism?

4. Marketing messaging—Are the marketing messages of the company steeped in pro-USA and American exceptionalism rhetoric, or are they heinously woke and anti-human and pro-scarcity? Do they celebrate America and freedom, or do they denigrate her and crap all over liberty?

5. Hiring policies for employees and vendors—Does the company hire the best man or woman for the job, or do they engage in woke racism and favor anyone but conservatives and straight, white males? Do they treat all employees and vendors as equals, or do they explicitly engage in harsh bigotry against conservatives and straight, white males?

6. Commitment to freedom in society—Does the company stand for American values, or has it been frightened into toeing the woke line? Do its political donations go to freedom-loving causes and organizations, as well as MAGA and non-establishment Republicans, or does it donate to woke, intolerant, and radical organizations (like BLM and Antifa), and Democrats and RINOS (Republicans-in-name-only)?

This "Freedom Scale" will be used to help patriotic consumers determine whether a company deserves their patronage.

Now to the book, "The Great Patriot BUY-cott Book!" We are proud of what we believe in. The media derisively calls us "far-right." We know exactly what that means—"so far, we've always been right!"

By the way, there is nothing "far-right" about our views. On every issue we believe in, polls show we are in the "Silent Majority." Most Americans are either "center-right" or so-called "far-right."

This book will start with chapters outlining what we believe in and what we believe patriots across America believe in. If you agree, if this sounds like you, then take action and buy from companies with similar beliefs and values, run by people who support our conservative and patriotic candidates and causes.

After those opening chapters that define what we stand for, then the list begins! We list 123 companies and media brands that we have determined are fellow patriots. BUY from them, support them, praise them, and pray for them.

It's time to stand up for America and the patriotic companies that stand with us.

God bless these companies, God bless patriots like you, and God bless America.

Wayne Allyn Root
Nicky Billou
1/1/2023

"The only condition necessary for the triumph of evil is for good men to stand by and do nothing."

Edmund Burke

What Patriots Believe

The next few chapters are a deep dive into what we both believe makes America great, why we love Her, and why She is worth fighting for. These are chapters written to make any patriot's heart beat faster, and to encourage patriots to band together to spend their money ONLY with other patriots!

The Patriot Parallel Economy

By Nicky Billou & Wayne Allyn Root

Trump-hating Meta/Facebook just laid off 11,000 people, equal to 13% of its workforce. The ultra-woke SalesForce.com laid off 8000 people, or 10% of its workforce, and even mighty Amazon just laid off 18,000 people, or 1.3% of its global headcount, with tens of thousands more to come in 2023. According to www.layoffs.fyi, a crowdsourcing website that tracks layoffs, over 1000 (woke) tech companies laid off employees in 2022, with even more layoffs to come in 2023. Victoria's Secret, a formerly awesome brand beloved by men and women, just fired their woke fool of a CEO, who wrecked the brand by focusing on plus size and male models. Bed, Bath & Beyond—aka the insanely woke company who banned the great patriot Mike Lindell's pillows from their stores—is about to declare bankruptcy.

As we speak, alternative, patriot economy pioneers are building out a new, more decentralized infrastructure for entertainment, tech, e-commerce and medicine that is already taking the world by storm. Conservative online companies like TheGatewayPundit.com, ZeroHedge.com, TheLibertyDaily.com, NaturalNews.com, breitbart.com, BonginoReport.com, DailyCaller.com, and DailyWire.com are leading the charge in creating alternative, conservative and patriotic entertainment. Others like Rumble, TruthSocial, Parler, GiveSendGo, and GETTR are among those in the vanguard of the alternative, patriot tech economy.

Nobody in the fossilized legacy media has clued into this yet. It's unbelievable how short-sighted they are! They're losing half (or more) of their audience (and studies show how this half of consumers spend the majority of the money).

What we are bringing you right here is going to give you a *huge (yuge!)* leg up on the macroeconomic factors that are going to transform the way non-woke people shop, consume products, earn incomes and engage with health and wellness providers. This is a seismic shift in the overall economy and the losers will be the centralized woke companies that have offended "The Silent Majority" (which is most of their consumer spending) by declaring their fealty to the twin insanities of ESG and LGBTQ/transgender ideology.

This is not a trend but rather a long-term transformation in how our economy will work.

The alternative conservative-capitalist-patriot economy brings people together to do business based primarily on philosophical alignment, rather than merely profit interests. My dad used to say that business is all about people, not money, and at the end of the day, that means that if your philosophical interests align, it is easier for your profit-motive-driven interests to align.

The Silent Majority (55% to 60% of Americans) are ready to make a conscious choice to stop most or even all their purchase transactions with woke companies like Disney, HBO, Target and Victoria's Secret: organizations that are increasingly coming across as anti-family, anti-child, anti-sanity, anti-freedom and just plain evil mixed with insane.

Woke brands will not be welcome in the patriot economy and will lose out, big time, on the explosion of new philosophically driven businesses. Their CEOs and boards will either pivot and jettison "wokism," or they will embody the phrase "go woke, go broke" and become the next Disney, losing millions of customers, billions of dollars in revenue, and tens of billions of dollars in their market cap.

2023 and beyond will showcase a widespread decentralization of online e-commerce. How? Through the rise of e-commerce hosting platforms that allow *anyone* to instantly set up an e-commerce front-end with 1+ million products already in inventory, fulfilled by network partners.

Businesses or vendors who are pro-Christian, pro-America and/or pro-freedom will be cancel-proof because woke platforms like Vimeo and Shopify will not be able to shut them down by blacklisting them. Why? Simple. Because these patriotic vendors will have workable alternatives for distribution and visibility through the patriot economy.

Patriot influencers, groups, and small businesses will be able to establish and launch their own e-commerce portals using these amazing new systems, and they will shift money away from the woke behemoths of e-commerce and into the pockets of regular patriot people at the community level. This new e-commerce-driven American Revolution will be much like the original American Revolution, with the behemoths playing the role of the British Empire, and the patriot influencers and businesses playing the role of the original "American Patriots."

The centralized warehouse model of early 21st-century e-commerce will contract sharply in 2023 and beyond with large layoffs, warehouse closures and big financial losses. In its place, smart investment money is now flowing into the new e-commerce storefront networks, backed by small local warehouses run by real people, not robots or "slave" wage workers.

The medicine and wellness industries will also experience a dramatic shift of dollars and customers away from the co-opted, centralized, corporate, pill-pushing doctors and sickness-pushing hospitals (most of whom banned effective miracle drug Ivermectin for Covid patients but were paid huge bonuses by the government and Big Pharma to literally kill their patients with the often dangerous drug Remdesivir and its deadly cohorts).

Instead, growth in these industries will occur in telemedicine operations that connect people with complementary, naturopathic, holistic, and alternative medical professionals who teach healthy solutions rather than push Big Pharma drugs, useless masks, deadly vaccines, expensive surgeries and dangerous "remedies" like chemotherapy and radiation (which often kill or cripple patients but make doctors and hospitals a fortune).

The net effects? HMOs and other behemoth medical organizations will become increasingly dis-intermediated, and more money will flow directly from wellness consumers (people) to actual healthcare professionals. Just as important, medical "licensing" will not be able to be so effectively weaponized by woke states like California to suppress the God-given and constitutionally protected free speech of doctors.

The rise of streaming is allowing patriotic filmmakers like Wayne's friends Kevin and Sam Sorbo; Nicky's friend Amanda Milius (**The Plot Against The President**), the daughter of the legendary patriot filmmaker John Milius (**Dirty Harry, Apocalypse Now**, and **Conan The Barbarian**); Nicky's friend Phelim McAleer (**Gosnell** and **My Son Hunter**); and Gina Carano (**The Mandalorian**); to reach massive audiences without needing to bend the knee to the woke Hollywood studios. Patriot filmmakers, who are making movies with traditional American themes, will eat woke Hollywood's lunch in 2023 and beyond.

Get ready to become a part of "the Patriot Parallel Economy," use it to "make the woke go broke," and reward the patriot companies, so that we have the resources necessary to take back America!

What Republican Voters Really Believe In—It's a Shame the GOP Has No Idea

A t least 74 million Americans voted for President Trump. Everyone I know believes the number was much higher. But we know for a fact 74 million Americans voted for Trump—because that's the number even the biased fake news media counts as fact. That's over 11 million more voters than the first time Trump was elected president in 2016—a record in the history of American politics.

This is the base of the Republican Party. And I know what these 74 million (and probably a few million more) voters believe in. How do I know? Because I've tested out my beliefs at many major GOP and conservative events where I was the keynote speaker.

The result? I got wild, enthusiastic standing ovations at every event.

What's amazing is that the GOP leadership in DC and the RNC has no clue what their own most loyal, passionate voters believe in.

But this is the raw truth. I'm here to spread the gospel. I'm here to report that "the truth will set you free." The people are desperate to hear the raw truth. Preach it. Let it rip. This is how you get standing ovations from tens of millions of Republicans, conservatives, patriots and capitalists. This is how you win elections.

When the media hears this story, they will get sick to their stomachs. So will the DC Swamp and the Deep State. Because they all failed. All the work they did was for nothing. No one believes their lies and fake news anymore.

I began my speeches with: "Here is what I know. Here is what I believe. Here is raw truth. Let me know if you agree by your applause. Only applaud if you agree."

I said, "No matter what the lying fake news media says, no matter what they try to stuff down our throats, I know President Donald J. Trump won the 2020 election."

Wild applause.

"I know Biden and the Democrats rigged, fixed and stole the election."

Wild applause.

"I know the more they ban, censor and forbid us from saying Trump won the election, their hysterical, illogical reaction is proof positive they stole it."

Wild applause.

"They think they destroyed Trump and demoralized us. The opposite is true. We love Trump now more than ever. We know Trump was one of the greatest presidents in our country's history. And we want him back. We'd walk over hot coals for him. After all your lies, fake news and fake polls, Donald Trump hasn't lost our support. And that's precisely why you hate him so much."

Wild applause.

"We know the perfect ticket in 2024 is Trump together with Florida Governor Ron DeSantis."

Wild applause.

"We know Voter ID isn't "racist." We know it's how you rigged and stole the election. With no Voter ID you used millions of fake mail-in ballots to steal the election in key battleground states."

Wild applause.

"We know no judge ever looked at the merits of our case. They feared for their lives. They knew liberal mobs like BLM and Antifa would burn the country down. They knew their own lives and the lives of their families were on the line if they overturned a presidential election. They knew the liberal mobs would try to burn their homes down. Their spouses and kids could never leave the house again without a police escort. Judges were scared to death. This was about intimidation, threats of violence, and mob justice."

Wild applause.

"We know Biden is not the real President. He's brain-dead. He has dementia. He's "a puppet.""

Wild applause.

"Who's in charge? We know Obama is the real president. He's back to finish the job. This is Obama's third term. But this time, he can throw caution to the wind. He can do it in the shadows with the puppet Biden as the front man. This time he has done more damage in a few months than in his first two terms combined."

Wild applause.

"And who is giving the orders to Obama and Biden? China and the Chinese Communist Party control Biden, Biden's family and the entire Democrat Party."

Wild applause.

"And we know the Mexican Drug Cartels are in charge of border and immigration policy. Democrat politicians are getting wealthy with billions in bribes deposited in offshore accounts, paid by the Mexican Drug Cartels and the Chinese Communist Party (who produce all the fentanyl). Democrats are making a fortune in kickbacks to keep the borders open. There is no other reason why anyone on earth would want open borders. Democrats are getting filthy rich."

Wild applause.

"And let's not forget Iran. John Kerry and the Democrats are desperate to restart the Iran treaty. Why? Because they're getting billion-dollar kickbacks in offshore accounts. These people are selling out America to get rich. They are traitors."

Wild applause.

"This is the most radical agenda in history. This is a communist takeover of the United States. The people running our country hate our country."

Wild applause.

"We know the Democrat (i.e., communist) game plan to destroy the USA is about open borders. They're inviting the entire world in. They want to destroy America, wipe out our votes, and make America foreign to Americans."

Wild applause.

"I know the next 9-11 terrorist attack is on the way through that open border. I know Covid-19, and the next pandemic, and third-world disease is coming through that open border. I know the collapse of the US economy is coming through that border. I know every migrant, every criminal and every welfare queen coming through that border is a future Democrat voter. And without Voter ID they all get to vote. They outvote the real American-born patriots like us. That's how Democrats are stealing this country."

Wild applause.

"And I know what we must do to the traitors who are destroying our country, opening the borders to criminals, disease and debt. And letting those criminals outvote us. LOCK THEM UP."

Wild applause.

"Who opens the borders in the middle of a deadly pandemic and ships illegal alien invaders across the country into our communities? Traitors.

Who tells everyone in the world to come here and get free healthcare while the cost of healthcare for the rest of us quadruples? Traitors.

Who names a border czar that fears visiting the border? Traitors.

Who tells illegals that while you're in our country waiting for an asylum hearing, our government will fly all your relatives into the USA, at the expense of the American taxpayer? Traitors.

Who wants to take the guns away from law-abiding American

citizens who have never committed a crime to leave us defenseless during the biggest violent crime wave in US history? Traitors.

Who doesn't want you to know that before Hitler killed 6 million of my Jewish people in Nazi Germany, the first thing he did was pass a law that Jews couldn't own a gun? Traitors.

Who doesn't want you to know that communist dictators murdered almost 100 million innocent people in the 20th century? That's direct murder. And hundreds of millions more starved to death. And how did they do it? They FIRST disarmed the people. Who does that? Traitors.

Who believes in "diversity," "tolerance," and "equality," but the only group that you don't allow to speak, post their opinions on social media, speak up at colleges, or have a job are conservatives and patriots? Traitors.

Who would teach our children at school that America is an evil country and white people are an evil race? Traitors.

Who would be dumb enough, ignorant enough, evil enough, and want to destroy the greatest country in world history, ever blessed by God? Traitors.

And communists."

Wild applause.

"We know the truth. You can never brainwash us. We will never stop fighting. We will never, ever, ever, give up, or give in. We will take our country back. God bless President Trump. God bless America."

STANDING OVATION.

Whether the GOP leadership in DC understands it, or not, THAT is what 74 million (or more) GOP voters believe in. That's raw truth that Republican voters are desperate to hear. Only the truth will save America. Only the truth will set us free.

That is how you get a standing ovation from Republican voters. And that is how the GOP wins elections again.

Treason: More Proof Biden is Owned Lock, Stock & Barrel by China

Afghanistan's tragedy and catastrophe are proof of my contention—President Biden, his family, and his Democrat puppet handlers are China-owned. They are doing China's bidding.

The Biden Crime Family is owned lock, stock and barrel by China and the CCP (Chinese Communist Party). Therefore, Joe Biden's stolen presidency is the best thing to ever happen to China.

I don't need to remind all of you what happened in Afghanistan. Everyone saw it. The question is, can you believe your own eyes? How could this happen? This is the worst debacle in US foreign policy history. And it threatens to become the worst catastrophic failure in US military history. Why? Because it was all foreseeable and preventable.

If only Biden and the Democrats were as good at foreign policy as they are at rigging and stealing elections. We'd be ruling the world instead of taking orders from the Taliban.

But all those American GIs dead and wounded (and all their devastated parents) isn't even the worst-case scenario. Biden is leaving Americans behind to fend for themselves. There is no way out. How many will be murdered? How many will be tortured and raped and starved? How many will be held hostage for a billion-dollar ransom? This is like shooting fish in a barrel. This is potentially the greatest PR scenario ever for ISIS.

I've warned for many months now that Biden is the most corrupt president in history. I believe he and his family are owned lock, stock and barrel by the Chinese Communist Party.

Since his inauguration, everything Biden has done, every action, every statement and every policy has weakened America and enriched China. None of this can be a mistake or coincidence. Joe Biden and his puppet handlers are Chinese-owned.

Let's examine the "mistakes" of Afghanistan. A picture emerges. These aren't mistakes.

First up, who evacuates the military first, leaving thousands of American citizens unprotected from blood-thirsty savages? Everyone knows you evacuate the citizens first, then the equipment, and the military. No one could be so stupid as to send the military home first. This was no mistake. This is TREASON.

Secondly, who leaves $85 billion dollars of military equipment on the ground? Overnight we just made the Taliban the 26th most powerful military in the world- with your taxpayer money. Who does that? No one is this stupid. This was no mistake. This is TREASON.

Third, who puts the Taliban in complete charge of security for American citizens? This is pure insanity. That would be like putting the Gestapo or SS in charge of getting Jews safely out of Germany. No one could be that naive. This was no mistake. This was TREASON.

Everyone involved in this decision should be arrested or court-marshalled. Tragically, Obama and Biden-appointed military leaders are too focused on Covid vaccines for an illness with a 99.7% survival rate; Critical Race Theory; climate change; purging all white conservatives from the military; and paying for transgender surgery.

Biden trusted the Taliban to protect our soldiers and citizens. Aren't they the enemy? Aren't they radical Islamic terrorists? Don't they execute people in the street? Don't they steal little girls to rape, enslave and marry? Weren't the good people of Afghanistan running for their lives for years from the vicious, bloodthirsty Taliban? But suddenly Biden made them our "partners?"

But wait, it gets worse. Biden gave the names of our citizens and Afghan allies to the Taliban to allow them through the gates of the Kabul airport. That's a "KILL LIST" for ISIS to hunt down all our own people. The US government has officially named the Taliban "terrorists." And Biden is handing the names of our citizens to terrorists? This is no mistake. This is TREASON.

What president would even consider leaving Americans behind to be murdered, or held hostage for ransom? This is no mistake. This is TREASON.

Who spends 20 years, trillions of taxpayer dollars, plus add in American lives and limbs, and then just runs away, so China can waltz right in, and take possession of all the lithium and rare earth minerals? No one is this dumb. This is no mistake. This is TREASON.

Every action Biden takes weakens America and enriches China. The open border; shipping Covid-infected illegal aliens all over our country; vaccine mandates; the budget-busting green infrastructure deal; killing our energy industry; paying millions of Americans not to work. Now add in the Afghanistan disaster. Biden is destroying America and helping China become the dominant force in the world.

And what just happened in Afghanistan will certainly lead to one more disaster: China will surely see this weakness as an invitation to invade Taiwan. Wanna bet? It's coming. Soon.

These aren't mistakes. <u>This is TREASON</u>.

Has Joe Biden Sold Out America to the Mexican Drug Cartels?

I told you so. It's become crystal clear I was right on the money. I've said for many years now on my national radio show that the best thing that could ever happen to the Mexican Drug Cartels would be a Democrat presidential victory.

This is their "rainy dream" (to put it nicely). Mexican Drug kingpins have waited their entire lives for this fantasy. They must be singing, dancing and toasting champagne in the streets of Mexico right now.

Because Joe Biden is the greatest gift ever bestowed upon the Mexican Drug Cartels.

Before Joe Biden decided to open the border, experts estimated the money made on drug trafficking by the Mexican Drug Cartels at around $500 billion a year. That's half a trillion dollars a year. Trillion with a "t."

Who quotes that figure? Republican Senators. See what Georgia Senator Purdue said in 2019: "At half a trillion dollars—$500 billion—that makes the cartel business and the drug traffic just in Mexico alone coming across to the United States bigger than Walmart, to put it in perspective. So, this is larger than our largest companies."

— Sen. David Perdue (R-Ga.), at a hearing of the Senate international narcotics control caucus, June 11, 2019

But that figure is bipartisan. Democrat Senator Dianne Feinstein quotes the same figure. Feinstein testified, "The illicit drug trade is a business, valued at anywhere between $426 [billion] and $652 billion."

That was all before Joe Biden's lax open borders policies.

But that's just drugs. What about human trafficking? Over 117,000 migrants crossed the US border in just the past month. Multiply 117,000 migrants times $10,000 each (the going rate for smuggling humans). That's well over $1.1 billion for human trafficking in a month for the Mexican Cartels. Now add in child sex trafficking. Days ago, a news report said cartels are selling little children at the border for $3,200 each.

So, what are the cartels willing to pay to keep the borders open and the dollars flowing? I'm a businessman. I always pay 5% to 10% "finders fees" to whoever brings me business. I'm sure it works the same way with Mexican drug lords, human traffickers, sex traffickers and pedophiles.

There's a lot of money on the line here. How much did Trump's strict border policies cost the Mexican Drug Cartels? Tens of billions? Hundreds of billions? By comparison how much extra money will Joe Biden and the Democrat Congress's open borders policies earn the Mexican Drug Cartels?

This is like Christmas morning for organized crime and terrorists.

Our country has clearly been sold out by Joe Biden and the Democrat Party. This is just pure common sense. Someone is getting filthy rich selling us out like this. The only real question is, how much is the Mexican Drug Cartel paying?

Don't take my word for it. The UK Daily Mail headlines just days ago screamed, "Mexico fears Joe Biden's immigration policies will help organized crime. Even Mexico thinks Biden is too lax on asylum. Mexican leader fears 'Migrant President' Biden will spark boom time for cartels."

Arizona border agents reported illegal immigration in 2021 has already surpassed all of 2018 and is on track to surpass 2018, 2019 and 2020 combined. Can you imagine how bad it was in 2022? Well, 2023 will be worse than all recent years in modern history COMBINED (because Title 42 is going away).

Trust me, it's going to get much worse. Millions more are coming. Maybe tens of millions. With Biden's Sanctuary policies, they can never be deported. And they can easily each bring in hundreds of their relatives and friends. So, everyone is on a fast track to citizenship. Everyone gets welfare, cradle to grave.

If this is allowed to stand, America is finished. The entire economy will soon collapse. America will be a foreign country…**to Americans**.

Now I ask you. Use your common sense. Why is this happening? Why would any sane president or political party want to encourage an invasion that will overwhelm our country and risk disease and death— let alone in the middle of a pandemic? This is insanity.

Why would we spend almost $100 billion to protect Ukraine from an invasion on their border, but refuse to finish a wall that costs only $25 billion to protect our own border?

Someone's getting filthy rich on this scam to destroy America. We know the Mexican Drug Cartels are making hundreds of billions. This is the dream of a lifetime for them.

But who's getting bribed inside the USA to allow this to happen? Who would you pay if you were a Mexican Drug Cartel kingpin?

I'm guessing the same group that sold out America to the Ukrainian mob and the Chinese Communists. And the same group that sold out America's uranium stock to the Russians. And the same group that sold us out to Iran with the world-class terrible Iran treaty.

It's Biden, the Biden family and the Democrat Party.

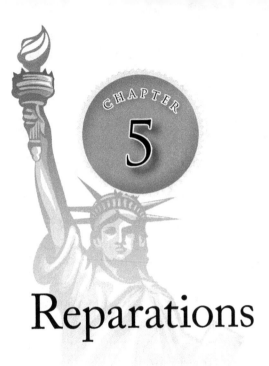

Reparations

Yes, it's true. I'm that Wayne Allyn Root. I'm the nationally syndicated conservative radio talk show host. A former conservative television host on Newsmax TV. And bestselling conservative author of 15 books- including **Trump Rules, The Ultimate Obama Survival Guide, Angry White Male, The Murder of the Middle Class** and **The Great Patriot Protest & Boycott Book.**

I'm the last guy you'd ever imagine coming out supporting reparations for black Americans. But it's true. I'm going to be the first high-profile conservative to support reparations.

Black Americans deserve reparations. Let's be honest. Look at their cities in ruins. Black inner cities in America look like Hiroshima and Nagasaki after the atomic bombs hit.

Have you been to any of them lately? Of course not. What sane person would take a chance of driving through Brownsville, Brooklyn, Crown Heights, Bedford Stuyvesant, Harlem, or the infamous South Bronx? Or how about Chicago's black South Side? How about virtually all-black inner cities in Detroit, Baltimore, East St Louis, Newark,

Oakland, Liberty City in Miami, Cleveland, New Orleans, Memphis, Atlanta, etc. The list goes on and on.

These places are synonymous with drugs, murder, violent gangs, and violent crime. Black cities and neighborhoods are a war zone. A black-on-black genocide. An American tragedy. Not to mention home-less tents, drug needles, poop, pee, condoms and garbage that litter their mean and hopeless streets.

Black lives do matter. So, yes, they do deserve reparations.

But who is to blame? It's sure **not** white Americans. Most of us have had nothing to do with the decline of black America. The vast majority of white Americans have never done a bad thing to a black person in their lives. We don't run their cities. We don't go near their cities. The destruction of black America has had nothing to do with us.

And none of us were alive for slavery, the civil war, or Jim Crow. My grandparents came to America in the 1920s. They lived in New York. They experienced their own prejudice and discrimination. My relatives had nothing to do with slavery, racism, or civil rights violations.

So yes, blacks are owed reparations. But who's to blame? There's only one common denominator: DEMOCRATS.

The Democrat Party and Democrat politicians are to blame.

It's the Democrat Party and Democrat politicians who should pay reparations. It's the policies of the Democrat Party that have led to poverty; misery; violent crime through the roof; theft of retail stores on a level never imagined; homelessness; hopelessness; rampant drug dealing and addiction; no fathers in black homes; burned out buildings, abandoned stores; lack of supermarkets; and streets filled with poop, pee, garbage, condoms, and drug needles.

A Republican on the streets of black inner-city neighborhoods is just a rumor. Outside of white cops, no whites go anywhere near those neighborhoods, let alone run them. Democrats run them 100%.

So, start with the DNC next time you ask for reparations for black America. Then knock on the doors of Obama, Biden, Kamala, Hillary,

Pelosi and Schumer. For good measure, you might also stop by the offices of Al Sharpton, Jesse Jackson and BLM. What have they ever done for black people? Nothing.

They scream, protest, threaten, intimidate, and even inspire hatred, rioting, looting, burning and murder. But when the dollars flow in from guilty white America, corporations, and the federal government, activist leaders like Al Sharpton, Jesse Jackson, and the founders of BLM get rich. But the black people living in those terrible conditions get little or nothing. Nothing ever changes with Democrats in charge.

And then there's the teacher's union. They get hundreds of billions of federal and local dollars. Black kids get nothing. Nothing ever changes with failing black schools.

So, yes, I vote for reparations. Let the Democrat Party and Democrat politicians pay. Along with the teacher's unions and BLM. Those are the correct groups to blame. These people are in control. They put you in these terrible circumstances. They should pay the damages.

Democrats owe black America. Democrats should be paying the reparations.

The Worst Racist in America

The story of racism is alive and well in America. Not just any racism. Really deep racism. Shocking racism. Racism so bad that it is unimaginable.

This is the story of a black liberal politician who hates black children. But the great news is, I know how to stop this. More on that in a moment. First, here is the incredible story of horrible black-on-black racism.

Washington D.C. Mayor Muriel Bowser is black, yet she recently demanded that the black schoolchildren of Washington DC either take the experimental, emergency-use-only Covid vaccine (against their will) or be denied an education.

Can you imagine if any white politician, let alone a white Republican, gave black children an ultimatum for any reason that might result in them being banned from an education? What would they call that white politician? "Racist. KKK. White extremist. White supremacist. Nazi."

But this isn't just "any reason" for banning a black child's education. The black mayor of D.C. is demanding black school children choose between their life and their education. We currently know two things about this experimental Covid jab:

Data from worldwide shows it is killing and injuring people at a rate never seen by any vaccine in world history. The same data from around the world shows that no child needs the vaccine. Children have a 0% risk of dying from Covid (unless they already have childhood cancer). But the risk of serious illness from the Covid vaccine is dramatically higher than from Covid itself. Perhaps up to 100 times higher.

The latest study was out just days ago. The study, funded interestingly by pro-vaccine interests, shows that at least 22,000 young adults must get the Covid booster jab to prevent one hospitalization.

https://dailysceptic.org/2022/09/07/covid-vaccines-up-to-100-times-more-likely-to-cause-a-young-adult-serious-injury-than-prevent-it-say-top-scientists/

Once boosted, that same study found young adults suffer up to 98 serious adverse effects from the Covid jab versus each hospitalization from Covid. In other words, the jab is far worse for young people than Covid itself. It is worse by almost 100 times. Mayor Bowser is playing "Russian Roulette" with the lives of Washington DC black schoolchildren.

https://dailysceptic.org/2022/09/07/covid-vaccines-up-to-100-times-more-likely-to-cause-a-young-adult-serious-injury-than-prevent-it-say-top-scientists/

One more interesting fact. The UK has banned Covid jabs for children under age 12. So have other countries. Yet in Washington, DC the Mayor is forcing children to take it.

Remember "The Negro College Fund"? Their famous saying was, "A Mind is a Terrible Thing to Waste." Here we are decades later, and a black mayor is denying black children an education. At the same time, she's forcing them to take an experimental jab that could kill or severely injure them. It sounds a lot like the Tuskegee Syphilis Experiment.

Martin Luther King is rolling over in his grave.

So, how do we defeat this terrible racism? The old-fashioned way—with lawsuits. It's time for a massive class action lawsuit by black parents in Washington D.C., who don't want their children persecuted for private healthcare decisions. And who doesn't want their children to have to choose between risking their life and getting an education?

Secondly, Martin Luther King believed in civil disobedience—such as strikes, boycotts and protests. Where are the black parents of Washington DC? Where is Jesse Jackson, Al Sharpton, Obama, or BLM? Don't black children's lives matter to BLM? Does a black child's education matter to Obama?

It's time for a strike. Every black parent in DC should keep their children home from school for a day to protest the forced jab.

And it's time for a "Million Parent March" of black parents in front of the DC Mayor's office to tell Mayor Bowser no tyrant has a right to deny a black child an education.

Now there's a Black Lives march that conservatives can get behind. I'm confident thousands of white conservatives would gladly march side by side in that mass protest against forced experimental vaccines.

Tulsi Gabbard
to The Rescue
of America

I never thought I'd be thanking an ex-Democrat Congresswoman and former Democrat Presidential candidate for telling the truth, exposing the evil Democrat agenda, and thereby giving much needed "ammo" and backbone to the cowardly GOP.

But Tulsi Gabbard just broke the mold.

Tulsi, we all love and appreciate you. Thank you from the bottom of our hearts for your courage, strength and honesty. You have done something that no one could even imagine before now.

You broke with not only the entire Democrat Party but also the DC Swamp, Deep State, and the evil cabal of Marxist Democrat donors like George Soros and Klaus Schwab of the World Economic Forum.

Tulsi just put the RINOS of the GOP establishment to shame, too.

Tulsi just exposed the purposeful Democrat plan to destroy this country. But remarkably, she just said it louder and with more raw truth than 99% of Republican officeholders and 99% of Republican candidates in this election.

Tulsi's exit statement in leaving the Democrat Party sounded like I wrote it. It was word for word, everything I've ever said on my national radio show, two national television shows and podcast for years—word for word.

We finally have a true Democrat insider who has witnessed and exposed the evil of the Democrat Party.

Tulsi didn't just say something short, sweet and meaningless—like, "I'm not leaving the Democrat Party. The party left me." She stuck a sword through their heart like a hero killing a vampire. She destroyed the Democrat Party like no former Democrat officeholder has in history. She explained in detail their radical agenda.

Tulsi's exit speech read like a Donald Trump or Wayne Allyn Root stump speech. First, she called Democrats an elitist cabal. She then admitted they had weaponized the government against conservatives.

She blames Democrats for wanting to kill free speech and send their political opponents to prison.

She reported Democrats are anti-white. In other words, she admitted Democrats are racists who hate white people.

She said Democrats are hostile to people of faith and want to take away our God-given freedoms.

She admitted Democrats have purposely opened the borders to destroy America.

She reported Democrats hate and demonize the police and openly protect and support criminals.

She said Democrats are a cabal of warmongers intent on starting World War 3 and bringing us purposely to the brink of nuclear war.

She said Democrats don't believe in a government of, by and for the people, but rather a government of, by and for the powerful elite.

She warned of the woke direction these radical extreme ideologues are taking our country.

And then she added in a media interview that Democrats are ushering in the "normalization of pedophilia."

All true. But…WOW. My jaw is on the floor. No former high-level Democrat official has ever said these words in history.

I've reported and warned about every one of these threats to our country for many years. So, what's the significance of Tulsi saying these same things?

First, she is the first Democrat Congresswoman and former Democrat Presidential candidate ever to admit any of this. That's credibility.

Second, she gives an "insider" account of what is happening in the Democrat Party at the highest levels. She is a witness. She proves what I've always warned—these are not mistakes, ignorance, or incompetence. This is all a purposeful, planned, coordinated, radical, extreme, communist, globalist, fascist attack on America.

Third, her words should embolden moderate and RINO Republicans to tell the truth about how bad this attack on America really is. 99% of Republican candidates have never gone this far, and never used words like this. They are cowards—scared of their own shadow. They're worried about what the media would say about them. Hopefully, Tulsi's words will embolden or shame them into telling the raw truth about what's really happening to America. Tulsi gives them cover.

Fourth, I argued that Tulsi's brave words and actions could inspire moderate, non-insane Democrats like Senators Joe Manchin of West Virginia and Krysten Sinema of Arizona to leave the Democrat Party. I was right. In, December 2022, Sinema left the Democrat Party to become an independent.

I hope that Tulsi is "the canary in the coal mine." She is the model. She has started a trend. She has started a tsunami away from the radical, insane, extreme, America-hating Democrat Party.

Tulsi then backed up her words by immediately endorsing several MAGA, America-First, Republican candidates for the 2022 midterms. I don't know if Tulsi is officially joining the GOP, but even if she chooses to remain an independent, this is certainly a great start.

Depending on what Tulsi does next (running for major office in 2024 as a Republican?), she could make a big difference in the direction of America. And she could inject some much-needed courage into the cowardly, weak, feckless leaders we have leading the GOP.

I hope she will inspire Democrat Senator Joe Manchin to join Senator Sinema and leave the Democrat Party.

Thank you, Tulsi. It's great to have you on my team. Welcome to "Wayne's World."

Here's How to Destroy Democrats: Make it Rain Illegals Aliens!

Mohammad Ali said, "It ain't bragging if you can back it up." So, I think it's okay to tout the fact that I've come up with quite a few ideas over the years that were adopted by prominent GOP leaders—including the President of the United States and now the best Governor in America.

I was the guy who recommended President Trump declare a "national security emergency" at the border—which would allow him to grab money from the Pentagon budget to build the wall.

I'm proud to report that liberals melted down.

I was the first to recommend President Trump should become

Speaker of the House if Republicans won the 2022 midterms. That way Trump could lead the impeachment of Biden and investigations into the DOJ and FBI. My interview with Trump on this topic made headlines all over the world. Sadly, Trump didn't want the job.

But still, I'm proud to report that liberals melted down.

Most importantly, over a decade ago, I wrote the column urging GOP Governors to ship illegal aliens to deep blue Democrat towns. If Democrats love illegal aliens so much, let them live with them. Over the years, I've repeated this idea hundreds of times on my TV and radio shows.

My idea was to ship illegal aliens by the thousands to exclusive, elitist wealthy towns and neighborhoods filled with rich, liberal hypocrites. And to the lawns of Democrat politicians.

Places like Martha's Vineyard.

Finally, someone had the balls and common sense to listen. Florida Governor Ron DeSantis just did it. DeSantis carried out both ideas. First, he shipped illegals to fancy Martha's Vineyard and to other Democrat cities. Then Texas Governor Abbott bussed illegals to the lawn of Vice President Kamala Harris's home. Bravo.

And once again, I'm proud to report liberals are melting down.

Why is the left going bonkers over just a few hundred illegal aliens being shipped to their fancy neighborhoods? Because this is a BULLSEYE. A grand slam home run. We've got them on the run.

The left is melting down over 50 illegal aliens shipped to a tiny island filled with wealthy liberal millionaires and billionaires (including Obama). But at the same time, they've claimed for years that Biden letting in five million illegals into America in his first two years as President is fine and dandy.

We've exposed liberals for the frauds they are. Democrats like John Kerry, Pete Buttigieg and Leonardo DiCaprio are screaming hysterically about "climate change" being the end of the world, while flying around the world in private jets emitting tons of carbon.

They want open borders. They want to wave millions of illegals into America. But the left doesn't want to live anywhere near them.

How bad is the meltdown?

California Governor Gavin Newsom calls for Republican Governors like DeSantis to be charged with "kidnapping" and face RICO charges.

Liberal filmmaker Ken Burns compares flying 50 illegals into Martha's Vineyard to six million Jews murdered in the Holocaust.

Democrat Governors are calling up the National Guard in panic.

DeSantis has hit a home run. I should know—after all, it was my idea.

But now we must double down. Put it into overdrive. Put the pedal to the metal. Every GOP Governor needs to join the fight. It's time for national expansion. We must "make it rain illegals" wherever rich liberals live.

First, don't stop at Martha's Vineyard. Let's hit all the rich, woke, liberal, spoiled brat, elitist Democrat towns. Send thousands of illegal aliens weekly to the Hamptons, Scarsdale, Great Neck, Beverly Hills, Malibu, Palo Alto, La Jolla, Napa Valley, Beacon Hill (in Boston), the Gold Coast of Chicago, the Upper East Side of Manhattan, Georgetown in DC.

Bury all the rich liberal towns with illegals. Make sure elitist, woke, liberal Democrat hypocrites have to step over hordes of illegals to get into Starbucks, their hairdresser, nail salons, supermarkets, restaurants, and their kid's schools. Make them scream, "Uncle."

Then let's go after the Democrat politicians.

Governor Abbott has the right idea to flood Vice President Kamala Harris's lawn with illegals. But don't stop there. Flood the lawns of every Democrat politician who supports open borders: Joe Biden, Nancy Pelosi, John Kerry, Chuck Schumer, clueless Transportation Secretary Pete Buttigieg, and send a few extra busloads to California Governor Gavin Newsom's mansion.

Let's see who the real "racists" are. If Democrats like illegals so much, you can live with them.

This is how we wake up America. This is how to make the issue of open borders bigger than life. This is how we expose Democrat politicians as elitist frauds and hypocrites. This is how we win a 2024 landslide.

How Different Would America Be Today if Trump Was Still President?

***NOTE: You can watch Wayne Allyn Root's TV interview with President Trump right here:

https://americasvoice.news/video/bwKm81tihPffI2X/

This is the easiest column I've ever written. It's so simple to imagine what America would be like today if Trump were still President. What a tragedy that we allowed a brain-dead, feeble, confused old man with dementia and diapers, and his radical, anti-American, globalist, communist handlers to destroy the greatest country in world history – in only 22 months.

Let's start with the obvious. How did this happen? The 2020 election was stolen. That's how they removed Trump from office and installed a man who doesn't know who he is, where he is, or what he's doing. A man who can't put two sentences together and who can't attract more than 20 people in concentric circles to his speeches—yet they want us to suspend reality and believe he got 81 million votes—the most in history. Bizarre.

And look what they did to us after rigging and stealing the election. They quickly put a plan in place to disassemble America; overwhelm the economy; make America poor; destroy the middle class; make America unsafe; and open the borders and make America foreign to Americans.

As a bonus, Biden and the Democrats put in place a disastrous foreign policy of liberal weakness, wokeness and appeasement that has set the entire world on fire.

Now World War 3 is upon us. Not just any World War, but a nuclear war that threatens to end the world as we know it. I warned about this for months. Even Biden finally agreed with me. He announced in the Fall of 2022 that we are closer to "nuclear Armageddon" (his words) than at any time since the Cuban Missile Crisis.

What a fine job you've done, Joe. And in record time!

Now let's look at exactly where we'd be if Trump were still President of the United States. And yes, I'm a pretty sharp and successful businessman- and I believe in every bone in my body that Trump is the rightful, 100% legitimate president. This should never have happened.

If Trump were still president...

We would have energy independence. We'd be selling our oil and gas to other countries worldwide. Gas would be $3 per gallon, and middle-class Americans would enjoy low prices and record prosperity.

OPEC would no longer have power over our lives, and we certainly would not be begging our socialist enemy Venezuela for an oil deal.

We would have low to zero inflation. Groceries would cost dramatically less than now. Middle-class consumers would be dancing in the aisles.

The stock market would be thousands of points higher. Trillions of dollars have been lost since Biden became president. All those trillions would be back in the hands of consumers, business owners and the retirement accounts of Americans.

Russia would have never invaded Ukraine. There would be no threat of World War 3 or "nuclear Armageddon". American taxpayers would have almost $100 billion in the bank (that's the money we've given away to President Zelensky and his Ukrainian mafia and Nazi cronies).

North Korea wouldn't be shooting rockets over Japan. Iran would be starved of funding by Trump.

The Taliban would not have $85 billion of our military equipment. And 13 US soldiers would still be alive, looking forward to Christmas at home with their families.

Our cities would not be destroyed by the worst crime wave in history—simply because Trump would never allow violent criminals to walk free while defunding and demoralizing police. A large percentage of police would not have retired in the past two years. We'd have plenty of cops to keep us safe. How many Americans, out of the tens of thousands murdered since Biden took over, would be alive and looking forward to Christmas with their families?

Britney Griner, the WNBA star in a Russian prison cell, was brought home by Biden in late 2022. But it was the worst trade ever. Biden left a Marine behind. Trump would have gotten them both back, or refused the deal.

There would certainly not be 87,000 new IRS agents hired to harass, intimidate and bankrupt the American people.

Although President Trump and I strongly disagree on the Covid vaccine, if Trump were still president, millions of Americans would never have been forced to take the experimental jab, or risk losing their job. Trump is strongly against mandates. He would never have forced one American to take the vaccine against their will.

How many Americans would still be alive or uninjured today, if never forced to take the vaccine by Biden's mandate? How many would still have their jobs?

I saved the most important for last—open borders. With Trump in the White House, we'd have a secure border. That means five million new illegals allowed in since Biden became president wouldn't be in our country. How many billions of dollars would be saved?

Think of all the criminals who have come in that open border. How many Americans murdered in the past two years would still be alive? How many communities and schools would be safer?

If Trump were still president, America would be a much nicer, wealthier, healthier and safer place. There'd be prosperity, with no inflation. We'd still dominate the world, instead of facing World War 3. America would be great again.

What a difference. Night and day. Life and death.

Democrats Are Border Crisis Deniers

emocrats call anyone who rightfully calls the 2020 election stolen, "election deniers." They call anyone who disagrees with their opinion of climate change a "climate denier." They are trying to evoke the "Holocaust denier" label. That's shameful.

But Democrats are the ones living in deep, dysfunctional denial. They are in denial of what anyone can see—crisis after crisis caused by Biden and the Democrats. Anyone can see the truth—assuming you're not blind, deaf and dumb. So, it's time to turn the tables. Throw it right back in their faces.

Democrats are "Border Crisis Deniers."

We are facing a dozen crises at our border. Unfortunately, they are impossible to miss.

We are facing an illegal immigration crisis and our nation is being overrun. Democrats can't see it. They are in denial.

We are facing an illegal alien crime wave in America. How many more innocent American children and cops must die before we acknowledge the crisis? Democrats can't see it. They are in denial.

There is an illegal alien gang crisis. MS-13 is filling our streets with cold-blooded killers. Parts of America—like Long Island, NY—are infested with MS-13 drugs and murders. They torture their victims before they murder them. Democrats can't see it. They are in denial.

There is a child sex trafficking crisis. How many children must be kidnapped and raped by drug dealers and pedophiles? How many children must be brought to America to become prostitutes? Democrats can't see it. They are in denial.

There is a drug trafficking crisis. How many more Americans must die of drug abuse and addiction before we act? More specifically, there are fentanyl and opioid crises going on at the same time. Opioids now kill more Americans than auto accidents. Democrats can't see it. They are in denial.

There is a prison crisis. Our prisons are filled with illegal aliens who have committed serious crimes like rape and murder. Why should we pay the bill? Billions of dollars are being wasted. That money could be better spent on military veterans. Or infrastructure. Or education. Democrats can't see it. They are in denial.

There is the threat of a disease epidemic. Whether it's Covid, or TB, or polio, or the next deadly pandemic, who knows what new diseases and tragedies are coming in through that open border? Are you willing to take the chance with your children? Democrats can't see it. They are in denial.

There is a humanitarian crisis. Women and children are facing rape, starvation and even death after the long journey. Experts agree one third to 70% of the women who take the journey are victims of rape. Democrats can't see it. They are in denial.

There is a welfare and national debt crisis. Millions of illegal aliens already in our country cost over $160 billion yearly in welfare, food stamps, court, police and prison costs. More come every day.

Democrats in New York and California are now promising Obamacare benefits to every illegal alien. Our national debt is over

$30 trillion. We are drowning in debt. A debt crisis that bankrupts this country is coming. Democrats can't see it. They are in denial.

There is a job and wages crisis for middle-class Americans. Illegals pouring through our open borders are taking jobs and suppressing wages by providing cheap labor. Democrats can't see it. They are in denial.

There is a terrorist crisis. How many terror cells have already gotten through our open border? What if one new 9-11 terror attack happens because liberals left the border open? Are you willing to take that chance? Democrats can't see it. They are in denial.

There is a pollution crisis. Studies show almost a billion people around the world want to relocate to America. What would that over-crowding do to our country? More people create more pollution, traffic, greenhouse gases, global warming, and filthy streets. Or don't liberals notice it if illegal aliens cause an environmental disaster?

Lastly, there is a voter fraud crisis. Democrats aren't in denial over this one. They know exactly what's happening. They want open borders because every illegal alien that comes into America is a future Democrat voter. This is the greatest example in history of "foreign interference" in US elections.

Anyone who can't see even one of these crises is in total denial. But if you deny all of them, you are either mentally ill; complicit in the destruction of America; or taking billions in bribes, kickbacks, and campaign contributions from the Mexican Drug Cartels. You pick.

But either way Democrats are "Border Crisis Deniers."

Biden Clearly Wants Civil War, Don't Take the Bait

D id you watch Biden's disgraceful speech in September 2022, from Independence Hall in Philadelphia, with the demonic red background? I did. And I instantly understood the Biden plan.

Although it's not actually "Biden's plan." Biden is a brain-dead puppet with dementia and diapers. Biden doesn't know whether Jill is his wife or sister. Biden is a walking cadaver who reads whatever script is put in front of him. Then Jill leads him off the stage, so he doesn't get lost. His handlers take him in the back, pat him on the head, hand feed him his baby food, and change his diapers. Then it's time to "put a lid" on Biden's day. It's time for a nappy nap.

So, none of this is Biden. Obama is the real president.

This is his delayed third term—and Obama is back to finish the job he started: the destruction of America, American exceptionalism, the great American middle class, and capitalism.

But Obama isn't the real order giver, either. He's just an order-taker. Obama carries out the orders he gets from the real psychopath-tyrants who control America: George Soros, Klaus Schwab of the World Economic Forum, Bill Gates and the Chinese Communist Party. China actually is the big dog. China gives the orders. China runs the show.

And it's clear what they want. That speech given by Biden was intended to incite civil war in America. Biden and his communist comrades want violence and a badly divided nation. They're daring us to start a civil war.

You know—exactly like all the BLM and Antifa events of 2020.

They want us to do exactly what they already did. Riots, looting, torching, robbing, murdering, attacks on police, $2 billion in damage, thousands of businesses destroyed—but with the media's protection, the BLM catastrophe was all forgotten.

They want conservative patriots to do the same—except this time, their business partners in the media will make us into "America's Most Wanted." They'll call us "Nazis, fascists, extremists, traitors, domestic terrorists, insurrectionists." Oh wait, Biden already called us all of that in his speech—before we've ever done a thing.

Can you imagine what they'd say if we actually committed mass violence? That's the trap.

What's their plan? Have you seen the polls? The working class and middle class of America despise Biden and his Democrat Congress. Biden and his comrades desperately want to hold onto power. Their goal is three-fold.

They want enough violence to instil fear and force most voters to stay home and vote via mail-in ballots. Then with no Voter ID or signature match, the Democrats can successfully rig elections and stay in power indefinitely.

Or, at the very least, they hope any violent act by conservative patriots will turn the voters against the GOP. They want you distracted, to forget the terrible damage Biden has inflicted on the US economy, and forget the issues that matter—inflation, sky-high gas and energy prices, sky-high grocery prices, open borders, vaccine mandates, and the death of the middle class.

Worst case extreme scenario, Democrats want to incite full-scale revolution or civil war, so they can declare martial law and suspend elections. Voila—they stay in power.

Democrats are going to lose badly if voters keep their eye on the ball. But if they are distracted; if they're turned against the "violent" Trump "America First" agenda; if they suddenly sympathize with "poor Joe Biden" and Democrats as "victims" of violence; if they fear civil war and insurrection by Republicans; suddenly everything changes.

Lastly, suppose the Democrats can incite civil war. In that case, they have the perfect excuse to send the military door-to-door to confiscate our weapons and arrest conservative leaders (whom they'll claim "incited violence and insurrection").

Without the fear of an armed citizenry, we're just another Australia. After that, they'll mask us, force vaccinate us, and lock us down forever. Until every small business is out of business. Until we are all living in poverty and misery. Until they have total control over our lives.

Then the communist attack succeeded. America is finished. The American Dream is dead. America is owned by China. We are all serfs and slaves.

That's the Democrat plan. Or more accurately, that's China's plan.

Yes, it's clear Biden and his handlers want civil war. Let's not take the bait. Let's not fall for the trap. They want civil war, but let's only give them civil disobedience.

Biden Is A Suicide Bomber

Our country is being destroyed. It's clearly a purposeful communist attack upon America from a thousand different directions. But the president isn't Biden. He is just the figurehead/puppet. The real president is Obama.

This is clearly the third term of Obama. His fingerprints are everywhere.

No president can legally serve three terms. Hence the need for a figurehead. Biden is just a "DDD"—a dummy with dementia and diapers. He says whatever is written on cue cards and signs whatever paper is put in front of him. That allows Obama to run the country from the shadows.

As long as they feed Biden his baby food, change his diapers and allow him to sniff little girls' hair, Biden does whatever his handlers tell him to do.

But Obama isn't the brains of the operation. Obama is just a communist tool. Obama takes his orders from a team of communist suicide bombers: Valerie Jarrett, Susan Rice, George Soros, Klaus Schwab, Bill Gates and of course, the boss of all bosses, the *capo di tutti capo*, China and the Chinese Communist Party.

Obama is owned lock, stock and barrel by the Deep State, United Nations, World Economic Forum and China.

The reason it's important to know Obama is the real president is that Obama was my college classmate at Columbia University, Class of 1983- where we learned the plan to destroy America.

That plan was called "Cloward-Piven."

Obama learned it well. It's happening today. Look around. The powers-that-be have just given it a different name: "The Great Reset."

But the goals are the same—destroy America, make us a socialist nation, make everyone poor and dependent on the government to survive, and make us into a one-party country (Democrat Party) with no opposition or dissent.

They are following the Cloward-Piven game plan to a T.

It's death by a thousand paper cuts. Under eight years of Obama, they "boiled the frog slowly." They attacked in slow motion, hoping you wouldn't notice. Then, like cooking a frog—they set the temperature so low the frog doesn't realize he's being boiled until he's dead.

But now, with Biden taking the heat, Obama is free to accelerate the process. So now Obama is throwing caution to the wind. He's set the heat as high as it goes.

This is the final communist takeover of America.

The biggest scams in world history are all being carried out all at once in front of our eyes. They're hitting you from so many directions, you're a combination of dizzy and punch drunk.

Here are the two biggest scams of all-time. These two scams are the foundation of this communist attack.

It all started with a stolen election.

That was number one. They had to remove Trump. They spied

on his campaign; then they spied on his actual presidency (which is treason); they trumped up fake charges to frame him; they spewed propaganda like the Third Reich; and they tried to impeach him multiple times over nothing.

When they failed at all of that, they stole the 2020 election.

Now they've weaponized the DOJ and FBI to raid the former president's home, ruin him, demonize him, bankrupt him, frame him, indict him for crimes he didn't commit, to prevent him from ever running again.

Trump scares them that much.

With Trump out of the way, there is no one to stop them. Now they're coming for you and me.

Secondly, it's all built around open borders.

That's the most deadly weapon in their toolbox. Open borders are the Democrat's "Nuclear Option." It's their Swiss army knife. It accomplishes everything at once.

It's simple. Just open the borders, invite the whole world in, and fill America with tens of millions of illegal aliens; the poorest people in the world who require welfare from cradle to grave; sick people with third world diseases who want free healthcare; and violent criminals—every country in the world sees this as an opportunity to open their prisons and send all their biggest problems to America.

That's how you sink the economy. That's how you explode the debt. That's how you overwhelm the system. That's how you make America a foreign nation.

And as a bonus, that's how you out-vote the legitimate citizens of America.

Just understand, the people in control of our nation are pure evil, and they won't rest until they've destroyed the greatest country in world history—and made you and me into serfs and slaves.

They are communist, fascist, globalist, Deep State SUICIDE BOMBERS.

UFC Vs. NBA: How To Build A Great Sports Brand Vs. How To Wreck One

By Nicky Billou

P rior to 2016, Americans could disagree on politics, but they were always united in their love of sports. That all changed when then-San Francisco 49er Colin Kaepernick decided to take a knee during the playing of the national anthem, and sports became fully politicized.

This trend was accelerated during the Trump years when NBA Champions, the Golden State Warriors, refused to meet with the President in the White House. Many other athletes in multiple sports began expressing their political views, usually in a culturally Marxist fashion, by denouncing the police, kneeling for the national anthem, and protesting against the US government, but remaining silent about the very real abuses by other nations' governments, especially if they had a financial interest in friendly relations with those governments.

LeBron James and his refusal to speak up against the government of Iran for murdering the brave world wrestling champion Navid Afkari and his deafening silence about the unrest in Hong Kong are prime examples of this.

Sports went from being a unifying force to being a divisive one. Athletes in the NFL, NBA, MLB and even the NHL began kneeling for the anthem. They adopted Marxist, anti-American talking points. They felt good about themselves for doing so.

A funny thing happened, though. The American people got pissed off. They stopped watching sports leagues that promoted woke ideology. As a result, the NBA's TV ratings cratered, and cratered badly. This was when Americans were locked up inside their homes and craving sports action to take their minds off the stress created by the pandemic and lockdowns. The NFL, MLB and the NHL also suffered rating declines, but not as severely as the NBA, mainly because they didn't embrace wokism as wholeheartedly.

But one sports organization bucked the trend, and did so in spectacular fashion, and that was the UFC, led by Dana White. White is a red, white and blue-blooded American, and he is having none of this wokist BS. He spoke at the Republican National Convention, and he endorsed President Trump. He stood up for Navid Afkari and begged the Iranian government to spare his life. He went on social media and pulled every favor he had to try and save the Iranian champion from an unjust execution. He failed, but he gave it his all, and unlike LeBron, he took a real chance to save an innocent man's life and didn't posture and preen to get the approval of the woke mob.

Dana White also kept his league going. He started holding fights almost immediately on Fight Island in Abu Dhabi and pushed hard to keep the sport going and give the fans some much-needed entertainment.

A funny thing happened. UFC ratings went UP! Pay-per-view fights also did very well, and interest in the sport is at an all-time high.

I was never a UFC fan before the pandemic. Now it's the only sports league to which I will give my money.

It looks like I'm not the only one.

Bravo, Dana.

Please, continue.

Why Does Everyone in the DC Swamp, Deep State, DNC and Even RNC Hate Trump?

Because They're All Power Hungry, Control-Freak, Evil, Slime-balls Who Hate YOU.

Now I'm going to "reverse gaslight" you. What does that mean? Well, "gaslighting" is when government bureaucrats, politicians, media, corporations and all the evil people in power lie to you; defraud you; smother you with propaganda; brainwash you; and try to convince you that what you see right in front of you...with your own two eyes...

is not true. That the lies they tell you are more important than the raw truth you can see right in front of you.

There are many ways and times you've been gaslighted in just the past few years. It's a stunning list.

The Deep State/DC Swamp/Democrats lied to you about open borders…they lied about Hillary's 30,000 deleted emails…they lied about spying on Trump…they lied about Russian Collusion…they lied about a perfectly fine Ukrainian phone call…they lied about massive Biden corruption in Ukraine and China…they lied about and covered-up the Hunter Biden laptop story that showed Joe Biden to be the most corrupt politician in US history…they lied about the origins of Covid…they lied about the need for lockdowns and masks…they lied about the need for Covid vaccines…they lied about the vaccines being "safe and effective"…they lied and covered up all the deaths and injuries from the vaccine…they lied about the success of miracle drugs Hydroxychloroquine and Ivermectin…they lied about Black Lives Matter (turning the worst riots and organized criminal anarchy in U.S. history into "peaceful protests")…they lied about the January 6th protests (turning a peaceful protest into an "violent insurrection" and "coup")…they lied about the clearly rigged and stolen 2020 election…and then they lied again about the clearly rigged and stolen 2022 midterm election.

You've been the victims of constant, severe gaslighting for a decade now. You're all part of a human psychology experiment in the limits that government and media can use in propaganda and brainwashing. At the same time, you can see they're lying right in front of your eyes.

And these are the same people telling you how terrible Trump is. How awful of a human being he is, what a criminal he is, what a danger to you, your family, and America he is, how unpopular he is and how he must be stopped at all costs.

I would not doubt by the time this book is out, the corrupt Biden administration, Deep State/DC Swamp and corrupt DOJ/FBI will have indicted and arrested President Trump.

Everyone in power and media is telling you, "Trump is bad, Trump is evil, Trump is unpopular, Trump is finished." Not just liberal media like CNN, MSNBC, the NY Times and Washington Post. But also, conservative media like Fox News, the Wall Street Journal and New York Post—all owned by the Rupert Murdoch family.

President Trump just declared he is officially running for President again in 2024. And all hell has broken loose. Everyone in power, everyone on the left and right, even the Murdoch family, has gone postal.

Trump is like kryptonite to the DC Swamp, Deep State, globalists, RINOS, Democrats, and the CEOs of the biggest corporations in the world. Trump is the one man standing in front of their plans to force vaccinate us to death; regulate us to death; tax us to death; digital ID us to control every aspect of our lives; move to a cashless society where every dollar you make is tracked; and worst of all, force us into a social credit score system that will make it impossible to travel, open a bank account, get a loan, or keep your job, if you disagree with the government's lies, misinformation and propaganda.

Trump can stop us from becoming medical experiments. Yes, I believe Trump, the man who supports the experimental Covid vaccines (mistakenly), is the one person who can keep us safe from them. Because he believes in freedom. He will never allow forced vaccine mandates on anyone—not children, government employees, military, or private sector employees. You know how many hundreds of billions of dollars that will cost Big Pharma?

So even though Trump supports the vaccine, Big Pharma hates him and needs to stop him, too.

And Trump is the one man who can stop China and the CCP. That's why they hate him so much.

Late in 2022, obsessed and extreme Attorney General Merrick Garland (the man who wanted the FBI to arrest parents at PTA meetings) ordered a special counsel to investigate President Trump. The powers-that-be will stop at nothing to destroy this man.

Remember, Trump created the greatest economy and stock market in modern history. He made all these people at the top filthy rich. They doubled and tripled and quadrupled their wealth under Trump. They should love him. Yet they all hate him. Why?

Because he's on our side. He's on your side. And he can't be bribed. So, he must be destroyed. They did it once by rigging and stealing an election where he got the most votes of any president in history; and the most votes of any Republican in history; and the most additional votes of any president in history.

Have you forgotten all this? I'm here to remind you. The American people love Trump. The evil people in power hate Trump. So now they're gaslighting you. They want you to forget all that.

Trump is our only choice. Why? Because the people in power hate him so much. They are all united to stop him because they're so desperate. Because they're frothing at the mouth against Trump and only Trump. No other GOP candidate seems to bother them or scare them.

That tells you all you need to know.

That's the tip-off. That's why there is no other choice. "We the people" have to unite to elect Donald J. Trump as the 47th president of the United States.

You've now been "reverse gaslighted."

Who Do You Vote For: The Easiest Choice in History

I t's so easy to decide how to vote in all future elections. You have to decide based on a few simple examples of what's going on in America right now.

You just have to decide if you love this country or hate America and want to destroy it.

Decide if being a conservative, Christian, patriot, or Pro-Life is a crime- because YOU could be the next one raided at 5 AM by an FBI SWAT team, and removed from your home in leg irons, in front of your children, for the crime of disagreeing with this administration.

Decide if you want parents harassed, intimidated and arrested by the FBI at PTA meetings for the crime of disagreeing with Critical Race Theory or transgender brainwashing.

Decide if you want your children to learn in school that this country is evil, our history is all evil, and all white people are evil...instead of the 3 R's.

Decide if you want to spend $10 a gallon on gas and $1,500 per month on your electric bill in the name of "climate change."

Decide if you want to soon pay $20 for a dozen eggs and $300 for a steak in the name of "climate change."

Decide if you will ride bikes to work and eat bugs for the rest of your life in the name of "climate change?"

Decide if you want to give up gas cars and only drive electric...while being told the electric grid is down, so you can't use your vehicle.

Decide if abortion "on demand," to the very moment of birth (and beyond), is more important than raging out-of-control inflation...a failing economy...your job...your assets, and savings...your retirement account...and putting food on the table for your children.

Decide if the Democrat answer to inflation is the correct one for you—a Democrat Congressman said in late 2022, "Just eat more Chef Boyardee." If that works for you, vote Democrat!

Decide if the definition of "science" means no debate allowed and anyone who disagrees with the government's opinion loses their job (including doctors) and the right to speak out.

Decide if you want to be masked for life if the government, or an unelected bureaucrat says so.

Decide if you want to be locked down for life if the government or an unelected bureaucrat says so.

Decide if you want to be forced to shut down your business (which pays your bills and puts food on your table) if the government or an unelected bureaucrat says so.

Decide if you want government, politicians, or unelected bureaucrats to force you to choose between an experimental vaccine or your job and income.

Decide if you want your innocent children to be forced to take an experimental vaccine if the government or an unelected bureaucrat says so.

Decide if you want to be suspended, banned, or "cancelled" anytime your opinion does not align with the government narrative, or it offends even one person.

Decide if you want the police to be defunded.

Decide if you want violent criminals (even murderers) to be let out without bail.

Decide if you want illegal aliens who are violent criminals, rapists, and murderers to be protected and kept in the USA.

Decide if you want 50 million new illegal aliens in America over the next 10 years and what that might look like. (P.S. This administration has let five million in, in just the first two years of Biden).

Decide if you want to go to prison or lose your life savings, for mis-identifying a pronoun that offends a transgender person.

Decide if you want your son to cut off his penis and become a girl at the age of six.

Decide if you want your daughter to shower in the locker room with 275-pound boys in pink dresses who identify as girls.

Decide if you want your innocent kindergarteners to go to school to see drag queen shows.

Decide if you're ready to be poor for the rest of your life because you're white and some white guys you never met 250 years ago mistreated black people.

Decide if you should be passed over for a job because you're white.

Decide if your kids should be denied admission to college because their skin color is white. Should we be guilty, shamed and punished for the rest of our lives for something that happened 250 years ago?

Take a drive this morning to any inner-city neighborhood, in any big city run by Democrats, and decide if you want your neighborhood, town and whole country to look and feel like that. Pay special attention to poverty and misery, homeless tents, drug needles, poop, pee, potholes, and the threat of dangerous crime everywhere. They are all run 100% by Democrats.

Decide if you support the U.S. military retreat and abandonment of Afghanistan, leaving thousands of Americans behind, allowing 13 American military heroes to die, and leaving $85 billion dollars of military equipment for our enemies.

Decide if you want your son or daughter to join the military if the top priorities are climate change, Critical Race Theory and protecting transgender rights.

Decide if you believe "swimming is racist." (An actual opinion uttered by the wife of newly elected Democrat US Senator John Fetterman).

Perhaps ask yourself this question—is there anything a white person can do that is **not** considered racist by a Democrat?

Decide if you like the idea of 87,000 new IRS agents to harass, intimidate and destroy every small business owner, working-class and middle-class American, and political opponent of this administration. Is this really America?

Decide if you'd get on an airplane if the pilot looked and sounded like Joe Biden (our illegitimate brain-dead president), or John Fetterman (our latest brain-damaged Democrat US Senator), or Rachel Levine, the gal who used to be a guy who looks like a guy with a really bad wig, who is one of the highest-ranking officials in the Biden administration (at Health & Human Services).

Would you get on the plane if they were the pilot?

Would you let any of them babysit your children?

Would you let any of them manage your life savings?

Then why are we letting them run our country?

This is the easiest decision in world history. If you're a patriot, if you're a parent, if you're a person of faith, if you have a job, if you pay taxes into the system, if you value free speech, if you value economic and personal freedom, if you have common sense, if you've seen up-close-and-personal what Nazis and communist thugs act like.

In all future elections, vote Republican like your life and your children's lives depends on it. Because it does, and they do.

"Freedom is never more than one generation away from extinction. We didn't pass it to our children in the bloodstream. It must be fought for, protected, and handed on for them to do the same, or one day we will spend our sunset years telling our children and our children's children what it was once like in the United States where men were free."

Ronald Reagan

Why We Believe Elections Are Being Stolen

The following few chapters are a deep dive into elections being stolen. As a young boy in Iran, Nicky saw a Presidential election being stolen. It happened when he and his father entered a polling place. A Revolutionary Guard soldier approached him and growled, "give me your ballot" and snatched it from his hand. He filled it out and stuffed it in the ballot box. He then said, "you can go now."

It's not that blatant here, but the Democrats have a long tradition of stealing elections (think about JFK and the mob stealing Illinois in 1960). And conservatives are not historically innocent of it, either (think about Jim Crow and the South—although those were Democrats, too). Today, all the election chicanery is being done by the Democrats, and we will shine light on that in these next few chapters.

Voter ID & The Woke War On Freedom & Free Elections

By Nicky Billou

O pposing voter ID is racist; requiring it is not. This is from a
Middle Eastern immigrant.

Last year, the state of Georgia passed a comprehensive election integrity bill, which expanded voting rights and access for legitimate voters, thereby making it easier for people to vote while requiring
voters to show ID before voting and securing the chain of custody for
mail-in and absentee ballots. Governor Brian Kemp said that the new
bill made it easier to vote and harder to cheat.

The wokist left went berserk, as did their allies in corporate America. First, they falsely smeared it as 'racist' and 'Jim Crow Part 2'. Then, Joe Biden got into the act and attacked it, too. They did not address the bill's merits; they just went on offense and attacked the motives of those who passed and supported it.

As a minority man with olive-brown skin, this makes my blood boil. The wokist left is so damn racist; they think men like me are too stupid to get ID to vote?! I need ID to board a plane. What's wrong with having ID to show you are a legitimate voter?

Mail-in balloting is fraught with fraud. That's why no other advanced democracy allows it, except in very limited circumstances. In most countries, if you want to vote, you must do so in person. France has outlawed the practice, with very few exceptions, as has Japan. In Canada, where I live, you must vote in person. You show ID before you vote. Both Liberals and Conservatives in Canada agree upon this. Liberals and Conservatives in the United States should also agree upon this.

Anyone who opposes election security and integrity is a supporter of tyranny, unfree elections and an intellectually dishonest gaslighter. Full stop. End of story. Conservatives need to persuade those in the middle that this attack on the Georgia bill is a monstrous fraud and is designed to weaken the American people's will to have elections they can trust.

Fully half the country has deep misgivings about the 2020 Presidential election. If those misgivings are not addressed, I fear for the country's future as a free Republic.

And to those corporate leaders jumping on the woke train, stop. You're about to alienate 60-80% of your customers. Do not wade into politics without knowing the facts and be smart and stop attacking the good people of this country with vicious and false smears. America in 2021 is not the Jim Crow South of 1921.

Far from it.

What makes America unique and special among world nations is that it alone engages in deep self-reflection, acknowledges its flaws, and addresses them forthrightly. Among these is the stain of racism. 100 years ago, being a racist was no big deal, in fact, a mainstream position. Today, being a racist is a very big deal and will get a person shunned and kicked out of polite society. This is a good thing. Americans today strive hard to be fair and deal with people based, not on the color of their skin, but on the content of their character. It is a far better and equitable place for it. Martin Luther King, Jr.—one of my heroes—would approve.

You've Been Gaslighted— Democrats Just Stole Another Election

When something is so obvious, if the outcome makes no sense or is literally impossible, then it is what it is. Forget "proof." You know it. You saw it. You felt it. You experienced it. It happened. It's real.

The 2022 midterm was just stolen. Just like 2020.

If you disagree, you're either delusional, terribly naive, or brain-dead. Or you're in on the fix.

It's time to admit we're all part of a massive experiment in fraud, theft, brainwashing, and gaslighting to a degree never before seen in world history.

Think of all the gaslighting they have done to you in the past few years. They lied to you about open borders, Hillary's 30,000 deleted emails and spying on Trump; they lied about Russian Collusion and the excellent Ukrainian phone call. They lied about the massive Biden corruption in Ukraine and China and about the Hunter Biden laptop. They lied about the origins of Covid, the need for lockdowns and masks and the need for Covid vaccines. They lied about the vaccines being "safe and effective" and covered up all the deaths and injuries from the vaccine. They lied about the success of miracle drugs Hydroxychloroquine and Ivermectin, and they lied about the stolen 2020 election.

You've been the victim of nonstop severe gaslighting for a decade now. You're all part of a human psychology experiment in the limits that government and media can use in propaganda and brainwashing...while you can see they're lying in front of your eyes.

And these are the exact same people now telling you Democrats just over-performed and stopped a GOP red landslide, against all odds, without cheating and stealing the midterm election.

Historically, every president in history facing their first midterm experiences a tough day, with automatically 20 to 30 House seats lost and four or more Senate seats lost. Still this unpopular President Biden is brain-dead with severe dementia and can't put three coherent sentences together. Yet Biden defied history?

While facing the worst economy in modern history, the worst inflation in America's history, out-of-control crime, open borders, failing schools and polls showing 75% of Americans believe the country is going in the wrong direction. Yet Biden beat all of that?

If you believe Democrats made a miracle happen, without cheating, rigging, and stealing, I have a bridge to sell you, over the Atlantic Ocean, in the Vegas desert.

First, every poll in the country showed a gigantic GOP landslide victory—ranging from red wave to red tsunami. Polls even showed women moved 32 points from September to October in favor of the GOP.

But in the end they all moved back to Biden and Democrats? Does that make sense to you?

Second, every poll in the country showed that the top two issues, by a mile, were inflation and the economy. And crime was in second place, along with open borders.

And they all voted for Biden and the Democrats? Does that make sense to you?

CNN's exit polls showed the GOP made massive gains among almost every voting group—men, women, white men, white women, blacks, Hispanics, and young people. Everyone.

And they all voted for Biden and the Democrats? Does that make sense to you?

In this environment where Americans can't afford gas, groceries, or rent because of an economy failing and inflation raging. People are scared to death of losing their jobs. Americans are living in cities plagued by violent crime, mass shoplifting, homeless everywhere and streets lined with feces, urine and used needles. Schools are failing and teaching your children to become masked transgenders.

In this environment, they all voted for Biden and the Democrats? Does that make sense to you?

They looked around at the disaster one man created in only two years, and they defied a century of historic midterm defeats for the party in power and voted for Democrats. Folks, you've been gaslighted.

But the actual proof the midterm was rigged and stolen is FLORIDA.

In Florida, the GOP won a landslide. DeSantis, Rubio and everyone else in the Florida GOP won in a red tsunami. The same one the polls showed was happening in the entire country.

Guess what Florida has? Florida has strict Voter ID, strict laws against voter fraud, severe prison terms for anyone caught trying to commit voter fraud, no mail-in ballots sent to every voter, no ballot drop boxes, no ballot harvesting, no ballots accepted for days after Election Day, no counting for days until the Democrat Party achieves the desired result.

Isn't it a funny and strange coincidence that in that state, with all of those strict rules against cheating, the GOP red tsunami happened as predicted? But everywhere else, where there are no strict laws against voter fraud, and they allow all that cheating, the red tsunami fizzled.

And that under-performance is being blamed on Trump? And on conservative MAGA candidates?

Yet in Florida, Governor Ron DeSantis is the most Trump-like, MAGA, America First, anti-woke, anti-trannie, in-your-face, ultra-conservative politician in all of America. And with that ultra-MAGA message, plus strict voting fraud laws, the GOP swept to a landslide victory.

And in most other places, they didn't. Coincidence?

Folks, we've been robbed. Again. This was a repeat of 2020. They've fixed, rigged, and stolen the election. First, they robbed us of the Presidency. Now they've robbed us of a red Republican landslide. And now they're trying to blame it on Trump.

This is gaslighting. And we've had our election stolen—again.

Has One Rigged Election Destroyed America Forever? The Odds Are Against Us

Folks, we are in a world of trouble.

America has faced tough odds before and beat impossible odds each time. We are resilient and relentless. We are a nation of people who believe nothing is impossible. So, never count us out. There is always hope.

But make no mistake, we are now in the fight of our lives. The odds may be worse than we have ever faced. Our nation is being destroyed from within by relentless and ominous attacks. America is hanging by a thread.

The nation is divided like never before. You'd have to go back to the Civil War to find our country this bitterly divided.

Our borders are wide open with millions of foreign invaders coming each year. The bad countries of the world are emptying their prisons—to send their worst criminals to us. Illegal aliens by the millions are bringing poverty, disease and violent crime; bloating our budgets; exploding our national debt; and destroying our education, healthcare and social security systems.

Inflation is raging like never before in modern history. No one really knows how bad it will get. And the government is hiding the actual level of just how out of control it is. More accurate measurements of inflation put us in the range of 15% to 20%. And it's only going to get worse. This has the potential to wipe out the great American middle-class.

If and when gas reaches $10 per gallon (or higher), the US economy will be at the point of collapse. What working-class or middle-class person can drive to work when it costs $200 or more to fill up one gas tank?

What will happen to the 3.5 million American truckers, whom each drive thousands of miles a week? If they can't get food or goods to market, our nation collapses into "Mad Max" territory. It's every man and woman for themselves.

And remember, we have the worst employee shortage in history. No one wants to work anymore because Biden gives so much government welfare and bailout money away. And I haven't even gotten to the worst scenarios yet.

But the point is a rigged election has changed everything.

Think of America with President Trump in charge. We had perhaps the greatest and most prosperous economy in history; the highest increase in middle-class incomes ever; the lowest unemployment ever—including the lowest black and Latino unemployment ever; inflation and interest rates at historic lows; a perfect supply chain—with a plethora of everything; and peace all over the world. But some Americans didn't like Trump's tweets.

What would you give to have Trump back right about now?

Everything is at risk now. America is a disaster now because we allowed Democrats to rig a presidential election. Utilizing millions of fake mail-in ballots with no Voter ID and little or no signature matching, plus an insane idea called "ballot harvesting" that used to be illegal in all 50 states; ballot drops in the middle of the night of 100,000 to 0 for Biden ballots counted for days after the election until the desired result was achieved. And every Republican witness was kicked out of the room while the votes were being counted in key battleground states.

No evidence of a rigged election there, right?

Now to the potential life or death problems we face because we allowed a rigged election.

We face the real possibility of World War III with the Ukraine-Russia war. Are you ready to let your sons and daughters die over Ukraine?

We face the real possibility of a nuclear war. We are closer than at any time in modern history. Even the UN announced that only days ago.

We are about to sign the Iran treaty—the worst deal in world history that hands nuclear weapons to the worst terrorist nation in the world.

China is almost certain to invade Taiwan—which makes up to 95% of the crucial computer chips in the world. Without them, we can't operate our computers, cell phones, or cars.

And then as a "bonus" we face financial collapse if we can't get enough oil to fill our gas tanks; if the Russian money we just banned from our system undermines credit markets and brings down our entire banking system; or if our dollar collapses as the "world reserve currency."

These disasters are not only all on the table at this minute, but what if several converge simultaneously? Then, our country, your life, and your children's future could be gone forever. Just like that.

All because we allowed a rigged presidential election in the United States of America.

And then we allowed it to happen AGAIN in the 2022 midterms. Or do you believe Biden defied the odds, all the polls, the exit polls, a century of historical trends for midterm elections, and the worst inflation, open borders, and crime wave in the history of America to have the best midterm results of any president in modern history? If you believe that, I have a bridge to sell you, in Vegas, over the Atlantic Ocean.

If we don't stop rigged elections, and if any of you ever again vote Democrat for anyone, for any office, you are officially suicidal.

P.S. "Let's Go Brandon."

"I just had my 11th interview with President Trump. He made it clear he will never mandate the Covid vaccine. Never. Ever. It's a free country. Trump can love the vaccine. I can hate it. But as long as no one is forced to take it, it doesn't matter.

If you want it, get it. Good luck. You'll need it. But I will never get it. I will encourage all my family, friends and fans to run away from it. That's freedom. That's what America is all about. That's why I'll always be in Trump's corner. He has my full support and confidence in 2024. We need Trump now, more than ever. MAGA!"

Wayne Allyn Root

We Believe the Covid Vaccine is Dangerous and Deadly. It Has to be Stopped. And the People Who Pushed It Must Be Held Accountable

The next few chapters are a deep dive into the so-called Covid Vaccine and the dangers it poses to people's health. Of course, woke, liberal, Big Brother "Branch Covidians," who practice the religion of "Vaccine-ology," and worship "the needle god," will have a fit upon seeing this. But vaccines take a decade to develop and test, with strict control groups (watched closely for a decade), not the few months this experimental Covid shot was developed in (with no control group).

And amazingly, governments all over the world pushed the misinformation that this shot was a vaccine (and then coerced or forced people to take it). It is not a vaccine. It has never fit the medical and scientific definition of "vaccine." It is a combination of experimental, for-emergency-use-only, jab and gene therapy. No one—including Big Pharma—has any idea (and they never did) what this vaccine will do to the innocent humans (including precious children) forced to participate in this evil experiment, for one year, two years, three years, five years, or a decade from now.

It's also important to note that international law prohibits forced experimental vaccines. We made sure this could never happen again with the Nuremberg Code. These Covid vaccine mandates were the most extreme violation of human rights since Nazi Germany.

The co-authors of this book believe in freedom. If you want this experimental jab, if you want to be a crash test dummy, do it. Good luck. God bless you. But the rest of us have the freedom to say NO. No one should have ever been forced (via mandate) to take the jab. No employee should have been forced to choose between their job (and income) and an experimental jab. No child should ever be forced to take this jab. No government has a right to trample parental rights.

The following chapters sum up our position. These were all adapted from columns/commentaries written by co-author Wayne Allyn Root over the past two years.

This is 1938. First They Came for the Unvaccinated

A uthor's Note: This chapter is adapted from a column Wayne Allyn Root wrote way back in 2021, when the unvaccinated were being persecuted, denigrated, and slandered. And the rest of America was being gaslighted with lies, fraud, and fake news about the so-called, "Pandemic of the unvaccinated." It was all lies that reminded Root (who is of Jewish descent) of Nazi Germany in 1938.

Wayne says, "This may be the most important commentary I've ever written."

It's time for alarm bells. It's time for me to play the part of Paul Revere. "The communist tyrants and dictators are coming. The communist tyrants and dictators are coming." They're coming first for unvaccinated Americans.

This is 1938. I'm a Jew. I now understand just a little of what it felt like to be a Jew in 1938. No, it's not the Holocaust. Nothing can be compared to the Holocaust. Ever.

But 1938 was not the Holocaust, either. It was the pre-Holocaust. It was the days before the nightmare when the foundation was laid to destroy the freedom, free speech, businesses and lives of millions of Jews (and others who disagreed with the Nazi government).

Everything happening today to the American people, to the US Constitution…to freedom…and in particular to unvaccinated Americans reminds me of 1938. This is only the beginning. It gets much worse from here.

First, "the papers." Vaccine mandates and vaccine passports today are like in 1938 when the Gestapo demanded "papers" from every German.

Republicans asked for "papers" from illegal aliens who had broken into our country. Nothing wrong with that. That's simply enforcing the law. That's merely keeping America safe from a foreign invasion. If you can't prove you're an American citizen, you are a criminal if you're in the country illegally. But Democrats said, "no, that's racism." If Republicans ask for "papers" once every two years for federal elections to prove you have a legal right to vote, Democrats say, "no, that's racism." To protect your nation, to protect your citizens, to protect your sovereignty, it's all "racism" to Democrats.

But now Democrats want American citizens, not illegal aliens, not criminals, but patriots born in this country, to produce papers 24/7. We'll need to show "papers" to enter restaurants, bars, nightclubs, gyms, concerts, casinos, conventions, hotels, and retail stores and to board a train, plane, or bus. We'll need to show "papers" to enter a supermarket or starve to death. All for the crime of being unvaccinated against, wait for it…

The flu.

It sure sounds pretty darn similar to the Gestapo demanding papers on the streets and at the train stations of Germany.

All for the crime of being unwilling to inject an untested, rushed-to-production, experimental, "for emergency use only, jab into our bodies".

What happened to the war cry of Democrats, "My body, my choice"? It only applies to killing babies (up to and even after birth), but it doesn't apply to dangerous experimental shots we don't want to be injected into our bodies.

Weren't Jews injected with experimental drugs by the depraved Nazi government? Wasn't that a key part of the Nuremberg trials? The Nuremberg Code states that no government could again inject experimental shots into the bodies of unwilling citizens. Isn't that a basic human right?

By the way, this isn't about vaccines. If you want the jab, take it. I won't stop you. I will try to educate you about the dangers and deaths. But I'd never limit your freedom, your choice. This is about vaccine mandates—forcibly injecting Americans who don't want it. That's 1938.

But there's much more in common with 1938—mask mandates. If you're scared, wear them. I'm not afraid, I don't want to wear them. Mask mandates force individuals to lose their freedom, choice, individuality, human rights (and oxygen). That's 1938.

Lockdowns are a match with the Warsaw Ghetto. Jews were locked down. Jews couldn't work. Jews couldn't travel. Jewish businesses were labelled "non-essential". If the government can force us to close our businesses, to kill our jobs, to decide who is "non-essential," then this is 1938.

Stars on clothing. Wait, it's coming. The vaccinated get into restaurants, bars, concerts, supermarkets, planes, and trains. They keep their jobs. The rest of us are marked as "sub-human" for life. That's the point of the star on your clothing. So, government and their agents can identify the dissenters. That's 1938.

Media and social media as the PR wing of the government. That's called "propaganda." Remind you of 1938? Back then Jewish books were burned. Today it's conservatives, patriots, and specifically, the unvaccinated. We are silenced. Our facts are labelled "misleading." Our websites are de-platformed. Our social media pages are banned, suspended, or shadow banned. Only "the facts" that agree with the big government's agenda count as "truth". That's 1938.

Door-to-door intimidation and making lists of those who disagree with "government knows best." Trust me, that army of door-to-door vaccine brainwashers will soon be turned into a Gestapo of gun grabbers.

1938 was the year Nazis banned Jews from owning guns. They took them away by going door-to-door. That's 1938.

As I write this, a former Obama Homeland Security official said the unvaccinated should go on "NO FLY LISTS." That's precisely how Nazis attacked the Jews and others who disagreed with their agenda. It was always "lists." Lists to be disappeared in the middle of the night, lists of those to be sent to re-education camps, lists of those to be sent to concentration camps, lists of enemies of the state. It's happening again. Maybe this time you'll only lose your job, or free speech. This is again 1938.

And it's happening. Millions of Americans are being de-platformed, banned, suspended, shadow-banned, kept out of stadiums, restaurants and stores, and losing their jobs, for the crime of being unvaccinated.

It's all disgusting and disgraceful. But I'm warning you, this is just the start. It's all going downhill from here. This is the beginning of the end of America. This is 1938. But soon to follow will be digital ID chips, social credit scores, a cashless society, and of course, vaccine passports for everything. Then anyone who dissents, who disagrees with the official government narrative or agenda (no matter how wrong, evil, or based on misinformation, lies, fraud and propaganda), will lose their ability to live a normal life.

Unless we stop it now. Unless we take a stand now. Unless we draw a line in the sand now.

First, they came for the unvaccinated. Trust me, next, they're coming for you.

Why Isn't Everyone in Florida Dead, or in the Hospital?

I hate to say, "I told you so." But yes, "I told you so."

I'm one of the few brave souls in the American media to warn and advise from day one (back in late February and early March 2020) not to ever lockdown the American people or the US economy.

I argued...

Lockdowns have never worked in history to stop a germ, disease, cold, flu, or pandemic. It couldn't and wouldn't stop Covid simply because you can't stop a germ.

There was never a reason to lockdown everyone. Anyone relatively young or healthy never had a reason to fear death from Covid. The survival rate is over 99%. But for anyone relatively healthy under the age of 60, it's near 100%.

Over time, lockdowns would cause more deaths than Covid—from suicide, depression, loneliness, drug and alcohol addiction, joblessness, poverty, and stress (from being unsure how to feed your family). And of course, no one goes to the doctor when the nation is shut down and in hiding. Their heart disease, diabetes, and cancer get worse or go undetected.

Worst of all, lockdowns would destroy the economy. If grandma or grandpa is sick or dying with Covid, how does it help them if their kids and grandkids lose their business, job, income, or home? It only makes things much worse.

I said from day one of the lockdowns (March 2020) that grandma and grandpa would not want their kids and grandkids to be jobless, hopeless, or homeless. That doesn't help grandpa or grandma. They want their kids and grandkids to live life and prosper. That's how you honor grandpa and grandma. You can't help them by ruining your own life, by closing your business, or by losing your home.

I warned the only way to fight Covid and pay for Covid, was to keep the economy open and healthy. And keep Americans employed.

Don't look now, but I was 100% right.

Florida is Exhibit A. Everyone needs to know the Florida story.

Florida Governor Ron DeSantis should be "America's Hero Governor." He stood strong in the face of massive pressure to close the state, close the economy, lockdown the people, order mask mandates. For the most part, he kept Florida open for business.

Now, look at the amazing results. Florida's economy is booming, people are happy, the quality of life is high, and very few are sick. It worked!

Even though Florida has been wide open for almost a year now (without mask mandates); even though Florida has the most retired senior citizens of any state (by far), Florida still has fewer deaths and hospitalizations than any of the know-it-all liberal lockdown states run by authoritarian Democrat Governors. Florida's numbers are better than New York, New Jersey, Pennsylvania, California, Michigan, Illinois, or any other deep blue state.

Florida not only has less death and hospitalizations, but the people of Florida kept their businesses open; kept their jobs; the kids all went to school; people kept on living their normal lives.

My friends own restaurants in Florida. Restaurants and bars are jammed. No one is wearing masks once inside. They tell me that not only are the customers healthy, but all of their employees are also healthy.

How is this possible? How can Florida be thriving, prospering and completely open for business? The kids in school while California and New York shut down for the entire time, businesses closed (in many cases, forever), jobs gone, schools closed, kids not learning a thing, yet the people of Florida are healthier?

The answer is simple. Democrat Governors blew it. They made all the wrong decisions. No lockdown was ever needed. Nor were they ever constitutional. No jobs should ever have been lost.

This was all a travesty. A tragedy. A farce. Florida is Exhibit A. Lockdowns don't work. People still get sick. You can't stop a germ. But lockdowns do succeed at three things—destroying the economy, destroying quality of life and ironically…

The stress, loneliness, depression, and poverty produced by lockdowns makes more people sick and more people die.

Lockdowns prove the cure is often worse than the disease.

The only solution is freedom and individual choice—let Americans choose whether to keep their businesses open, or go to work, or wear masks.

As usual, the government was wrong. The government made things much worse. As usual, liberal Democrat ideas failed miserably. Lockdowns are perhaps the worst mistake in America's history.

Case closed.

Debating the
Dangers Of The
Covid Vaccine

I t's so easy to win a debate with an ignorant liberal. They have no facts. They have no brilliant oratory. Just name-calling. After my national TV interviews last week explaining how the Covid-19 vaccine is killing and injuring thousands of Americans, I received an email from an ICU doctor. He called me a "moron." Below is my reply filled with common sense, logic, facts and most importantly, real "SCIENCE" about the dangers of the Covid vaccine. Needless to say, the doctor never replied.

Dear David,

First, I read & answer all my own emails. I'm answering you personally. I don't engage in ignorant terms like "moron" towards people that disagree with me.

Second, this country (and the world) is filled with both unvaxxed and vaxxed who are sick with Covid-19. It's a nasty and contagious flu. At this moment almost every vaccinated person I know is sick with Covid. In Germany over 96% of those with Covid are vaccinated. In Denmark over 90% with Covid are vaccinated.

Third, study after study from around the world shows that the Covid vaccine damages and weakens the immune system, thereby making it more likely that the vaccinated will get sick with each successive variant.

Fourth, if the vaccine is so great, why do the deep blue states like NY have massive Covid outbreaks? New York City just set the all-time record for Covid infections in a day, of any city in the world. New York right now has almost 30% of all the Covid cases nationwide. How could this happen if vaccines, masks and lockdowns worked?

Fifth, if the vaccine is so great, why are there far more Covid deaths in 2021 with the vaccine, than 2020 — without it?

Sixth, as a MD, why don't you pay attention to the VAERS reporting system? It's been the gold standard for decades to identify if any vaccine is causing more harm than good.

This Covid jab—according to VAERS—has killed over 21,000 Americans. That's separate from the cardiac arrests, strokes, blood clots and permanent disabilities. And this jab has caused a staggering 1 million "adverse effects." These numbers are from VAERS—compiled by CDC.

Seventh, are you aware Columbia University researchers found that VAERS is vastly under-reported? They say you must multiply by 20 to get the accurate number of deaths and injuries. So according to the math of Columbia U. researchers, there are actually over 400,000 deaths and millions of injuries directly from the vaccine.

How could you doubt VAERS? Pfizer's own research showed 1,200 deaths from the initial first few weeks of their vaccine rollout. That's Pfizer's reporting.

Anyone who wants the vaccine should get it. It's called choice. They should thank President Trump for the availability of this vaccine.

The rest of us who are relatively healthy and/or relatively young have a 99.9% recovery rate from Covid. No one should be FORCED to vaccinate, mask, lockdown, lose their job, or close their business in America. We have choice. We take risks every day.

Certainly, everyone should agree, no baby, toddler, child or teen should ever be forced to take this jab. As a John Hopkins study proved, the risk of a child dying is literally 0. Out of 48,000 childhood cases of Covid they studied, no healthy child died.

I've had Covid. It was gone in 48 hours after I took Ivermectin, plus antibiotic (Z Pak), plus mega doses of Vitamins C, D3, Zinc and quercetin. Plus, I received intravenous Vitamin C. Worked like a charm. Gone in 48 hours. Mild.

I now have immunity. No one with immunity needs to vaccinate. The risks far outweigh the benefits. I make healthy lifestyle choices. I'm not anti-vaxx. I'm pro-immune system.

In India, the government ended the worst Covid outbreak anywhere in the world, by handing out free packets of Ivermectin plus vitamins. Covid went away literally overnight. Deaths dropped to virtually 0. That's exactly what America should have done and should be doing right now.

There are dozens of studies around the world proving the efficacy of Ivermectin and HCQ as anti-virals to defeat Covid.

I wish you well. I hope I've opened your eyes to the alternatives out there. I know what you see each day in your ICU—the sickest of the sick. It's tragic they have no access to Ivermectin or HCQ, plus vitamins like C, D3 and Zinc. Early treatment (in the first 3 to 5 days) with this combination would almost guarantee few ever wind up at the ICU—where you see them—and it may already be too late.

It's important to allow different opinions and questions. If "science" won't respect or allow discussion, or debate, it's no longer science, it's just propaganda.

I'm doing my best to keep America healthy. I know you're doing your best.

God bless.

If the Vaccine is So Great, Why are So Many People Dropping Dead?

AUTHOR'S NOTE: Believe it, or not, this chapter is a replay of a column I wrote in early 2021. Yes, I had a crystal ball way back then. Think of where we are today. Everything I reported and warned about here is happening today—on STEROIDS! Make sure your seat belts are fastened!

NEWS HEADLINES:

Heart Attacks Skyrocket, Young Children Suffer Heart Problems, Soccer Players Dropping on Fields, ICUs Overwhelmed From Coast to Coast

The Covid vaccines are clearly causing a global health disaster.

There are so many warnings from all around the world. I'll list just a few in this column. But the U.S. media remains silent. They're as quiet as a church mouse. Why?

Japan's Health Ministry just announced that "the Moderna and Pfizer Covid vaccines could cause heart-related side effects in younger males." Health experts in Japan have witnessed skyrocketing rates of myocarditis and pericarditis in young men and teenagers. And they've seen the same nonstop heart issues with middle-aged Japanese and seniors.

All over America, and all over the world, cardiac arrest, heart inflammation, and heart attack deaths are exploding. Young athletes are dropping right on the field; star soccer players in Europe are dropping dead in the middle of games; referees, coaches and even fans in the stands are having cardiac emergencies. It's something no one has ever seen before. It's an epidemic.

What do all these victims have in common? They've all been vaccinated.

In America, the media is filled with reports of hospital Emergency Wards and ICUs overwhelmed with seriously ill patients. From coast to coast, there are so many sick people lined up, there aren't enough beds or nurses. Sick patients are lying on gurneys along the hallways. Doctors and medical experts call it a "mystery" why so many Americans are sick. They can't understand what's happening.

But I can solve the mystery. These are Covid vaccine injuries overwhelming ERs and ICUs. The very illnesses that are most prevalent in this mysterious health emergency—heart attacks, cardiac arrest, strokes, blood clots, multi-organ failure—are all the same Covid vaccine side effects listed in the VAERS report (Vaccine Adverse Event Reporting System).

What a coincidence.

But it's not just in the USA. It's happening everywhere. In the UK, the Evening Standard newspaper reports that up to 300,000 British citizens are facing sudden heart-related illness and cardiac arrest.

UK medical experts are blaming PPSD—"post-pandemic stress disorder." 300,000 Brits couldn't possibly be dying and crippled from the vaccine? Of course not. They're all nuts. It's all in their heads.

These brainwashed Kool-Aid drinkers can't see what's right in front of their faces. Or perhaps doctors, scientists and researchers are too afraid of losing their medical licenses or multi-million-dollar government grants to speak up.

In the case of the media, it's all about greed. Big Pharma buys a large proportion of the ads on every TV news network in America. If the media offends Big Pharma with stories of vaccine deaths and injuries, Big Pharma would pull their advertising campaigns, and the media would lose billions of dollars in revenue. Half the newsroom could be fired.

Not to mention the stock prices of these same media companies would collapse (due to the loss of revenues). There go the retirement accounts of Lester Holt, Don Lemon, and Rachel Maddow (and every employee in the newsroom). Everyone knows where their bread is buttered. So, the truth is hard to come by.

So, what's the truth? All anyone with a shred of credibility, morality and decency has to look at is a few key factors.

First, the FDA has just announced that they need 75 years to fully release the Pfizer Covid vaccine data. If I told you to "Trust me, I'm selling the world's best health tonic, but I can't disclose any of the test results or ingredients for 75 years until everyone asking is dead." Would you trust me? Would you buy what I was selling? Would you inject it into your body?

Second, a federal judge demanded that Pfizer release some of that data immediately. Just in the first few thousand pages (out of millions), detailing results from the first few weeks of vaccines, Pfizer admits in their own data that their vaccine killed 1,223 Americans and produced 42,086 adverse effects. Among the most prominent adverse effects were heart attacks and heart problems.

Third, the VAERS system is reporting 19,886 deaths from the vaccine and just under one million adverse effects—including tens of thousands of hospitalizations, crippling injuries and permanent disabilities. That's just in America. The EU numbers are even higher.

Now let me let you in on a terrible secret. My insider healthcare sources report that so many victims are filing reports with VAERS that the system is hopelessly overwhelmed and backed up. There may be 20,000 or 40,000, or 60,000 more deaths waiting to be processed into the VAERS system. They tell me the numbers are staggering. But those deaths aren't listed at VAERS yet.

Now you know why hospital ERs and ICUs are overwhelmed with people seriously ill.

So, my question is, shouldn't someone be investigating this escalating health disaster? Shouldn't someone in the media be reporting on this unimaginable tragedy? Should politicians be protecting us?

One thing I know- something very bad and very evil is happening.

Here is Who is to Blame for the Deadly Covid Vaccine Disaster and Cover-up

E very day, it becomes clearer what a disaster the Covid vaccine is. Data from all over the world is showing proof that those who are vaccinated are much sicker, more often hospitalized, and dying in far higher numbers than the unvaccinated.

In both Europe and the USA, the mortality data clearly shows a massive, never-before-seen-in-world-history, increase in non-Covid deaths since literally the day the vaccine mandates started.

In the beginning, I was one of the only radio and TV hosts in America, pointing out what a disaster this was and how terrible the early results were. But I sure was feeling mighty lonely. Most conservative TV and radio hosts went along with the fraud. Of course, their networks were paid millions of dollars to cover the deadly results from the Covid vaccine.

Now suddenly everyone is waking up from an almost two-year slumber. The lightbulbs are going off. Even most conservative hosts were fooled at the start of this pandemic and vaccination program. They should have followed Ronald Reagan's famous warning: "The 9 most terrifying words in the English language are: I'm from the government and I'm here to help." That was the tip-off. The government is never the answer, it's usually the problem. Oftentimes, government is searching for solutions to problems that don't exist (to make itself look more important). Government feels your pain because they're the ones causing it.

Whatever the government says, I assume, is a lie, or wrong, or propaganda, or in their best interests, but never mine.

I'm glad my fellow conservative hosts are waking up. They are all great people and great patriots. They did nothing wrong. They were lied to. They were fooled by propaganda from our government, CDC, FDA and Big Pharma. I'm thrilled they've seen the light. I'm glad we're all back on the same team.

But please always remember, I was there from the first day, warning of the dangers of an experimental, for-emergency-use-only jab that was never properly tested and never had a life-and-death-necessary control group. I'm proud to report that I knew from the first day that everything the government was demanding was wrong (lockdowns, masks, vaccines), and I never caved to pressure or accepted payoffs to shut up. I stood my ground. I stood up for my fellow Americans (and conservatives). I risked my career and income to do what I knew was right.

When everyone around you is vaccinated and dying, I guess there comes a point where it's hard to avoid admitting there's a disaster going on. So now even the media and a few brave Democrats are starting to talk about vaccine deaths and injuries. But guess who they're blaming?

Democrats live by the saying, "Never let a good crisis go to waste." So now they're just starting to blame President Trump. Right now, it's a trickle. Soon it will be a tsunami. My gut says as the deaths multiply, this will be the new Democrat talking point moving forward.

It's hard to avoid what's happening now. The deaths are accelerating. Everyone sees it, and it's impossible to ignore. So many Americans are dying "suddenly." That includes celebrities, athletes, rock stars and even doctors.

But it's more than just death. Many Democrat politicians are walking zombies after vaccination—look no further than the zombie twins President Joe Biden and Pennsylvania US Senator John Fetterman. They can't even put two sentences together anymore. First, Fetterman was bragging about being vaccinated, then suffered a major stroke. Those two prominent Democrats speaking on a stage together are like a combination of "Weekend at Bernie's" and "Night of the Living Dead."

So now that everyone sees what's happening—from heart attacks, strokes, blood clots, and dramatically rising levels of Stage 4 cancer to mass "sudden death," it's clear they're going to blame it all on Trump. I'm here to tell you that Trump is not to blame.

Here is who is to blame...

Dr. Fauci gets 100% of the blame. First, he funded the research that led to Covid. Then Fauci conned the nation, long after he knew the vaccine didn't work. Fauci saw the CDC-compiled VAERS list of deaths and injuries from the vaccine piling up, and he saw the vaccine trial evidence that many volunteers in the trial had died. Volunteers were injured, crippled and disabled; pregnant mothers lost their babies at an alarming rate. Yet Fauci covered it all up. Even worse, he encouraged more Americans to get the vaccine, knowing the terrible side effects of this tragic experiment gone bad.

The CDC and WHO get 100% of the blame. They knew everything Dr Fauci knew. Yet they pushed the vaccines. And then later, after everyone with a brain saw the death toll, they recommended these death shots for children. So, these organizations are guilty of mass murder on a scale not seen since WWII.

Biden and the Biden administration get 100% of the blame. They certainly knew about the rising death and injury numbers by March of 2021, when Biden gave the orders to OSHA to mandate the jabs at every large corporation in America. They condemned millions of American employees to risk death or terrible injury.

Every Democrat Governor and member of Congress gets 100% of the blame. They all drank the Kool-Aid, like the suicidal followers of maniac Jim Jones at Jonestown in Guyana. Except this time, it wasn't just 909 people who died. This time, the Democrat vaccine cult led millions to death and serious injury.

The media is 100% to blame. They are the PR wing of the Democrat Party. They covered up this entire massive tragedy. This is the biggest healthcare debacle in world history. And the media has covered it all up, blacked it out, whitewashed it. Oops. The big question is, who bribed them? Were they paid directly by Big Pharma? By the Biden administration? Or did they get insider stock info and make billions of dollars betting on the Big Pharma stocks? Maybe all of the above.

The whole mainstream media sold out. I'm guessing the biggest conservative talk radio syndicators sold out, too. They all took millions to shut up. They agreed that no host, or guest, could tell the truth about vaccine deaths or injuries. They took blood money. They sold out all of YOU - their customers.

Google, Facebook, Twitter, YouTube, Instagram and virtually every social media site run by the kings of Silicon Valley are 100% to blame. They all sold out for their piece of gold. By banning and censoring any mention of vaccine deaths or injuries, they were a gigantic part of this mass death conspiracy. The big question is, who bribed them? Were they paid directly by Big Pharma? By the Biden administration? Or did they get insider stock info and make billions of dollars betting on the Big Pharma stocks? Maybe all of the above.

Doctors across America are 100% to blame. They knew. They saw their patients dying. But they were too greedy, or perhaps scared of losing their license to speak out. The doctors played dumb. They were sheep. They accepted the lies of the CDC, WHO, FDA and AMA without asking any questions. They called that "science."

I suspect Bill Gates, Klaus Schwab, George Soros and other anti-American globalist billionaires who were desperate to stuff "The Great Reset" down all of our throats are to blame. However, I'm unsure if we will ever know their full role in this tragedy.

Big Pharma and the vaccine manufacturers are the worst of all. They knew from day one. They saw the vaccine pre-trial results. They buried the tragic and deadly results. They demanded complete 100% immunity from lawsuits. Then they demanded that the vaccine trial results be kept secret for 75 years. Now we understand why.

Then there's the global culprit—China is responsible for all of this. They started the ball rolling. It's clear China purposely sent Covid-19 our way to destroy our economy, plunge America into depression, destroy Trump's re-election and overturn Trump's victory in the trade wars.

Then there's President Trump. The man, the Democrats want to stop at all costs. The frontrunner for the 2024 presidential election. The man they've tried to destroy since the day he announced for president. The man they illegally spied on. I've lost count of the man they've tried to frame so many times. And now they want to frame him for the Covid vaccine gone wrong.

It won't work. Trump was the CEO of America. He's not a doctor, scientist, or medical expert. He was lied to by Dr. Fauci, Dr. Birx, the CDC, the FDA and a bunch of evil, greedy Big Pharma executives. Trump was defrauded just like the rest of us.

Trump's only job was to act as CEO and Five Star General to get America and the US economy back on track. To save tens of millions of jobs. To save capitalism. Of course, he was a cheerleader for the vaccine. Of course, he pushed to get it past the finish line. That's any CEO's job. But Trump didn't create the vaccine. He didn't manufacture the vaccine. He didn't conduct the vaccine trials. Nor was he part of the cover-up of the trial results.

The so-called "medical experts" and media are responsible for the biggest disaster in history, lying to President Trump, committing fraud against the people, then acting in conspiracy to cover it up. Trump was taken advantage of, just like the American people. They defrauded us all, and these criminals are responsible for mass negligence, leading to mass murder, and then mass fraud, to cover-up the truth.

It's not "Trump's vaccine". People are dying from the vaccines all over the world. So, is it "Trump's vaccine" in the UK, Scotland, Portugal, Netherlands, Israel, or Canada—where some of the worst vaccine death data are being reported?

More importantly, Trump was against vaccine mandates from the first day. That would have protected millions of American workers whom Biden forced to choose between their jobs and the vaccine. With Trump as President, no mandate would have ever been allowed. Not one American would have ever been forced to take the Covid jab. How many employees of large corporations would be alive today if Trump was President? How many members of the military? How many policemen, firemen and nurses? How many pilots?

So, desperate Democrats who conned and forced the American people into taking a deadly experimental vaccine can try to blame Trump, but that dog won't hunt. Democrats praised the vaccine, and Democrats mandated millions get the death shot. Democrats slandered anyone who told the truth, and Democrats called reports of vaccine deaths and injuries "misinformation". The Biden government and their militarized agencies (like the FBI) worked hand-in-hand with social media companies to suspend, censor and ban any mention of vaccine problems, injuries or death.

The Biden government paid hundreds of millions of dollars to media companies (including conservative media) to ban anchors, hosts, or guests from ever mentioning a bad word about the vaccine. Did you know that?

This is their debacle. This is their disaster. This is their Waterloo. Blaming Trump is just one more expansion of the world's most insane political witch-hunt and gaslighting.

Trump was the CEO of America, trying to save lives, save jobs, save the US economy, and save capitalism. But NEVER was he going to force the vaccine on a single American—adult, child, private sector employee, government employee, or military member. Trump believes in freedom. And that works for me. I'll bet it works for 80+ million Trump supporters and voters too.

But...

Now is the perfect time for President Trump to come out and say, "I was duped. I was lied to. Dr. Fauci, Dr. Birx, the CDC and the FDA lied to all of us. I am so sorry to admit that the vaccine is a failure. It doesn't prevent Covid. It doesn't prevent the transmission of Covid. And it appears many people have been affected adversely—including death. I was told it worked. I was told the side effects were minor. I was told the vaccine trials showed it was safe and effective. I know now those were all lies."

"Based on what we know now, it's clearly time to suspend the vaccine program and investigate what went wrong. And if found guilty of fraud and cover-up, demand everyone involved be criminally prosecuted. We must clean house at the CDC, FDA, WHO, AMA and other government agencies that allowed this disaster to occur. To make sure nothing like this ever happens again, Congress must pass a law that bans mandates for any experimental or emergency-use vaccine or drug. No one should ever force any American to choose between their job, or their life. Or to choose between going to school or college, and their life."

Do that Mr. President, and you're the President of the United States again in 2024. Case closed.

Seven Dead Doctors in 14 Days Don't Lie: The Covid Vaccine is a Killer

AUTHOR'S NOTE: Here is another commentary author Wayne Allyn Root wrote long ago. Yet because of the gaslighting and cover-up by the mainstream media, few Americans to this day know about the many deaths of young doctors in Canada in general. Or more, specifically, the unimaginable cluster of doctor deaths in July of 2022.

Have you ever heard of seven doctors dead in a 14-day period (from July 13-July 28, 2022)? How about five dead doctors in one city (Toronto) in a few days? How about 14 dead doctors in the past nine months? And these dead doctors were mainly YOUNG.

https://www.theburningplatform.com/2022/07/30/five-physicians-four-50-or-younger-have-died-in-the-toronto-area-in-the-last-two-weeks/

Do these headlines catch your attention? Because they're all true. Confirmed. Fact. It just happened in Canada—a small country of 37 million (one-tenth the size of America).

In Canada, they're obsessed with the Covid vaccine. The government is ruthless to the point of being criminally insane. If you don't get vaccinated, it's difficult to live a normal life. And you absolutely can't practice medicine anywhere in Canada.

And they don't count you as vaxxed if you took one or even two Covid vaccines. Nope. In Canada, you need four vaccines.

Virtually everyone is pressured to get vaccinated. There is no choice, if you want to avoid arrest, keep your money, keep your dog, keep your job, and participate in society. I think there's a country music song in there somewhere!

So, we know all Canadian doctors are triple or quadruple vaccinated. That's a certainty.

And yet we also know five doctors died in a few days in one city—Toronto (where my co-author, Nicky Billou, lives). FIVE.

We also know that seven Canadian doctors died in one 14-day period.

We also know 14 Canadian doctors (at least) died in the past nine months. One of my heroes, Steve Kirsch, just wrote about this development.

https://stevekirsch.substack.com/p/fourteen-young-canadian-docs-die

Steve is a lifelong Democrat mega-donor to the Democrat Party who has changed to Republican because of all the vaccine injuries and deaths. Despite donating $20 million to Democrats, he tried calling many Democrat Senators and congressmen (to whom he donated) to inform them about all the vaccine deaths and catastrophic injuries. They wouldn't return his calls. He recently appeared on Tucker Carlson's Fox News show to talk about it.

https://thevigilantfox.substack.com/p/fox-news-cant-verify-steves-data

Back to all these dead doctors. Mostly young dead doctors. Have you ever heard of anything like this? Of course not, because it's never happened in my lifetime. I'm guessing it's never happened in history. Perhaps it happened during the Plague in the Middle Ages (also known as the "Black Death").

Maybe we should start calling the Covid jab "Black Death II".

Did you know about any of these dead doctors? Of course you didn't. It's been a total media blackout. Why would five dead doctors in one city be worthy of media coverage? Or seven dead doctors in 14 days in one small country? Nothing to see here. Just move along.

Canadians are freaking out. The shrieking noise on social media got so hot and heavy that a Canadian newspaper was forced to publish a story. A Toronto hospital was forced to admit in that newspaper story that five young doctors had, in fact, died. But they warned readers not to jump to conclusions. The vaccine had absolutely nothing to do with it.

Of course, the vaccine had nothing to do with it. And Bill Clinton never had sexual relations with that woman. And Joe Biden says we're not in a recession. And Biden also says inflation is now 0. And the Afghanistan pullout was flawless. You can always trust those in authority to tell the truth, right?

Something is very wrong. The vaccine is killing, crippling and disabling thousands per week. Deaths in the United States are skyrocketing higher than ever seen in history. So many of these victims are dropping dead "suddenly" and "unexpectedly." Those are the words in almost every obituary nowadays.

They've even developed a name for it—SADS (Sudden Adult Death Syndrome). One day they're perfectly healthy, and the next day they died in their sleep, they died in the middle of a business meeting; they died while swimming; they died while driving; they died while playing sports.

Heck, last week, a Saudi Ambassador dropped dead in the middle of a speech right in front of the TV cameras.

https://nypost.com/2022/08/10/saudi-businessman-muhammad-al-qahtani-dies-mid-speech-in-shocking-video/

And then there's the dramatic explosion of cancer. Rare cancers.

Fast-growing cancers. Stage 4 cancers. And these victims all happen to be vaccinated (most of them with the booster).

Does this seem normal to you? Have you ever seen this before in your lifetime? The government knows what's happening. The CDC knows. The life insurance companies know—they can't afford the massive losses. The funeral homes know—business is booming. The honest doctors know—they're just afraid of losing their licenses if they go public. Big Pharma knows—the deaths and injuries were reported in the vaccine trial data that they tried to keep secret for 75 years.

This vaccine is a disaster. It's time to stop the vaccine before there are no doctors left. And then, who will be left to treat the millions of victims who are vaccine injured? Think about that.

Seven dead doctors in 14 days don't lie.

Finally, One Honest Doctor Comes Forward to Report the Death and Devastating Injuries From the Covid Vaccine

I t's really that bad. The Covid vaccine is clearly the worst medical experiment and healthcare disaster in history. The results are all around us. Just tune into the news. Or sports. Or TMZ. Celebrities, athletes, even doctors are dropping dead left and right. In numbers never seen before in history.

Why not ask the life insurance executives if you don't believe me? Since the vaccine, they're reporting death rates up dramatically (from 20% to 40%). These are non-Covid deaths. This is a number never before seen in history. Even during World War II, deaths were not up by 20% to 40% across the USA. Not even close.

Recently, I reported on my personal experience. So many of my friends are dead, are dying, or are very sick since the Fall of 2021. It's a "cluster" of cancer, heart attacks, strokes, serious illness, and death—but almost strictly among the vaccinated. My unvaccinated friends are healthy.

Then just days ago, I reported on seven doctors who died suddenly in Canada, in 14 days. All are not just vaccinated, but based on Canadian mandates, almost certainly quadruple vaccinated. But, in that remarkable list, are five dead doctors—all young—in just a few days in one city—Toronto.

But the real issue is the ones who aren't dead from the Covid vaccine, but are injured, crippled, or disabled. Instead, they'll have to live in pain, misery and poverty for the rest of their lives.

Based on what a "trusted source" just disclosed, we are in for a world of trouble. A credible doctor has come forward. He/she wants to remain anonymous for fear of losing his/her medical license for telling the truth about vaccine injuries.

Let's call this doctor Dr. Smith. Let's say he/she practices on the East Coast. As a podiatrist, his/her practice is over 60% older (65 years old and above). Dr. Smith believes that about 95% of his/her patients are vaccinated. The results are devastating.

The unvaccinated patients are fine - no major illnesses or problems. But Dr. Smith says over 80% of the vaccinated patients are very sick since vaccination.

What is Dr. Smith seeing? First, the vaccinated are dying off. Secondly, he/she's seeing heart attacks, strokes, and blood clots in incredible numbers. Third, they're getting rare and advanced (Stage 4) forms of cancer. Many of his/her patients were in cancer remission, but suddenly, post vaccine it has come roaring back—except now it's spread everywhere in their bodies. He/she used to see skin cancer once or twice a month, now he/she sees it several times a week. Thyroid cancer has skyrocketed—and it's always after they get the booster jab.

They're suffering from terrible neurological diseases—such as Parkinson's Disease. They're experiencing terrible shingles outbreaks. They're suffering serious intestinal issues—like colitis and diverticulitis.

He/she has never seen before—so many of his/her patients experiencing terrible eye issues. One patient went suddenly blind in one eye while driving. He/she's also seeing more elderly patients falling than ever before.

After hip or knee replacement, Dr. Smith's patients used to recover quickly. However, if vaccinated, they often experience terrible post-operative complications and need to be hospitalized.

After seeing or hearing about all these injuries Dr. Smith always asks, "What's changed? Are you doing anything different? Are you on any new medications?" The answer is always "Nothing new, but I just got my Covid booster shot."

Then there's the issue of aging. Dr. Smith's older patients have aged horribly, literally overnight—since being vaccinated. They feel it and say it themselves. They say, "I'm falling apart." "I've aged so badly in the past year—I feel like I'm 100 years old." "What's happening? I feel so old. Nothing in my body works anymore." But everything worked fine one year ago. They were aging slowly and beautifully. What changed so radically? They were vaccinated. It's been all downhill since.

Finally, just today one of Dr. Smith's older patients announced that his 4-year-old great-granddaughter has cancer. He was devastated. Dr. Smith asked, "Was she vaccinated?" The patient replied, "Yes, why do you ask?"

No one gets it. It's as if everyone is either brain-dead, clueless, delusional, or brainwashed. The signs are everywhere. How many of you know someone who was vaccinated and died or suffered a bad illness soon thereafter?

We all do.

Wake up, America. This Covid vaccine is the worst medical experiment and healthcare disaster in history.

And here's the frightening part—this is just the beginning. The vaccines only started in 2021. As time goes by, it's only going to get much worse.

Will All of Hollywood Soon Be Either Dead Like Ray Liotta, or Paralyzed Like Justin Bieber?

I 'll get to Justin Bieber and Ray Liotta in just a minute...
But first, I want to explain why I know and understand liberal Democrats who worship "the vaccine god" better than any conservative in America.

It's because I've known nothing but liberal Democrats all my life. I grew up on a dead-end street on the Bronx borderline, in a majority-minority city. I attended an almost 100% black middle school, then a 90% black high school. Almost everyone I knew was a Democrat.

I grew up Jewish, attended synagogue and was Bar Mitzvah-ed. Almost every Jew I knew was a Democrat—from my rabbi to my childhood friends, to my own uncles and aunts.

I was accepted to Columbia University, one of the finest Ivy League colleges in America. Forget Democrats, most of my professors and classmates bragged that they were socialists, Marxists, or communists.

I became the host of five television shows on Financial News Network (now known as CNBC). Everyone I met in journalism, broadcasting and the media was an ultra-liberal Democrat.

I lived for 13 years in Malibu, California. Everyone I met in Malibu was an ultra-liberal Democrat.

One more unique tidbit—I'm a lifelong health food and vitamin enthusiast. For decades most of the people I met in vitamin stores were liberal Democrats.

So, I've been living and working around liberal Democrats, socialists, Marxists, and communists my entire life. I may understand them better than any conservative or Republican in America.

Most of the liberal Democrats I met in my life were cynical; anti-establishment; never trusted anything politicians or the government told them; hated and distrusted Big Pharma; and were almost always anti-vaccine.

Most of the Birkenstock crowd I met in vitamin stores and health food stores would not allow their kids to be vaccinated. Most of the liberal mothers I met over the years (and I lived in Manhattan, the Hollywood Hills and Malibu—so I know liberal mothers) did not trust vaccines and believed vaccines caused autism.

So, how did we get here?

Because right now, at this moment in time, liberal Democrats, and assorted socialists, Marxists and communists (who make up the Democrat Party)...and in particular everyone in Hollywood and entertainment...have spent the past two years in a spell...a mass psychosis...a Stepford Wife trance...a Jim Jones of Guyana-like, Kool-Aid drinking, mass brainwashing event.

The liberal Democrats I knew my whole life were mostly atheists.

But suddenly, every Democrat I meet believes in a "god." They've all found religion. Their god of choice is the Covid vaccine. Their religion is "Vaccine-ology."

They love Vaccine-ology so much, many of them switched from Scientology.

The liberal Hollywood crowd is filled with addicts—drug addicts, alcohol addicts, sex addicts—but now their addiction of choice is the vaccine needle.

Instead of AA meetings, soon they'll be attending VA meetings—"Vaccine Anonymous."

Suddenly every liberal Democrat in Hollywood loves Covid vaccines like Christians love Jesus. They worship the needle. They are desperate for boosters for their boosters!

Suddenly Democrats ask no questions—they trust everything Big Pharma tells them. They still hate capitalism, yet Big Pharma committing fraud and covering up vaccine injuries and deaths to make trillions of dollars and turn Big Pharma executives into billionaires, doesn't bother them in the slightest.

If a brain-dead zombie puppet with diapers and dementia (i.e. Joe Biden) tells them the vaccine is safe, they just roll up their sleeves and say, "Your wish is my command. Hit me with your best shot."

Hollywood limousine liberals want to place "the great Covid vaccine god" on the back of our coins. "In Vaxx We Trust."

Funny, but doesn't this sound a lot like what happened under Stalin…and Hitler…and Castro…and Rev Jim Jones in Guyana?

All over the world athletes, politicians, actors, rock stars and celebrities have been "dying suddenly" or suffering cardiac arrest, heart issues, strokes, blood clots and massive increases in cancer—all since 2021 and the advent of the vaccine. Athlete deaths are up over 1700%. FIFA (pro soccer) deaths are up fivefold—almost 100% are heart-related.

Millennial deaths are up by a staggering percentage since the vaccine. The worst of any group. Why? Because they're working age. They were forced by mandate to take the Covid jab or lose their jobs.

And like clockwork, as I wrote this chapter, the data came out that since February 2022 in Canada, 4 out of 5 Covid-19 deaths have been vaccinated. Keep in mind that those are just deaths from Covid-19 itself.

That doesn't include deaths among the vaccinated from a heart attack, stroke, blood clots or cancer. So, the Covid vaccine doesn't even prevent death from Covid, while destroying your immune system.

The numbers are shocking. Ask any life insurance executive, or funeral homeowner. Ask any cardiac nurse. Study the VAERS report.

But now it's hitting home in Hollywood. Days before I wrote this chapter, one of my favorite actors, Ray Liotta, died in his sleep on the set of his latest movie. Was he vaccinated? Almost certainly. No actor can get on a movie set without proof of vaccination.

*NOTE: Obviously, I'm not a MD. I can't state for sure that Ray Liotta, or any other celebrities, actors, rock stars, athletes, and politicians died or suffered heart attacks or strokes directly from the Covid vaccine. But I am an opinion commentator. And it is my opinion that the vaccine is the likely suspect. And we all have a right to ask questions. We all have a responsibility to try to save future lives from this slow-motion train wreck. We all have every right and reason to ask for investigations.

Then only days later, 28-year-old superstar singer Justin Bieber went public with his face paralysis—from a rare disease called Ramsay Hunt Syndrome (a virus in the shingles family). Bieber was forced to cancel his tour. Shockingly, his 26-year-old wife had a mini-stroke "unexpectedly" only weeks before.

These are medical conditions that mimic vaccine injuries happening all over the world. So were Bieber and his young wife vaccinated? Almost certainly—his fans are not even allowed to attend his concerts without proof of vaccination.

*NOTE: Obviously, I'm not a MD. I can't state for sure that Justin Bieber or his young wife, or any number of other celebrities, actors, rock stars, athletes, and politicians died or suffered heart attacks or strokes directly from the Covid vaccine. But I am an opinion commentator. And it is my opinion that the vaccine is the likely suspect. And we all have a right to ask questions. We all have a responsibility to try to save future lives from this slow-motion train wreck. We all have every right and reason to ask for investigations.

All over the world, vaccine injuries and deaths are piling up. Hundreds of studies from around the globe report that the Covid vaccine damages the immune system and results in dramatic increases in heart attacks, heart inflammation, strokes, blood clots, cancer and terrible outbreaks of shingles and facial paralysis.

Liberal Hollywood has lapped up the lies, misinformation and world-class cover-up by the government, media, and CDC like no other group in the world. You can't step on a set or stage in Hollywood, or anywhere the entertainment industry, without proof of vaccination.

Bieber and his wife are the tip of the iceberg. Soon we'll see and hear about a tsunami of Justin Biebers and Ray Liottas. Which star is next?

The question is, in this celebrity-obsessed world, what famous celebrity's death will be the tipping point that wakes the world up to this unfolding tragedy?

*NOTE: This is an opinion chapter. These are my opinions. These are public figures. In a free speech society, we have every right to ask questions and request investigations of an issue that could affect the future health and lives of millions of Americans.

I've Figured Out the Whole Covid Vaccine Scam- Here It Is. Read it and Weep.

I finally figured it all out.

We are in the middle of the biggest scam and "get-rich-quick" Ponzi scheme in world history. Some might call it mass murder on a grand scale. Open your eyes—see the remarkable number of famous actors, politicians and athletes who are dropping dead, or suffering heart attacks, strokes, blood clots, and dramatic cancer increases. Is it coincidence?

Recently, we've seen so many famous actors and rock stars die.

Is it all coincidence? Is it all about "old age?" Or is something terrible happening that needs to be investigated? Why are so many famous people dying? Why are so many of them dying relatively young?

Could it be because lots of average people are dying too? Life insurance executives are reporting non-Covid deaths are up a staggering 40% across the USA—the most significant increase ever seen. Ask any funeral home director—business is booming like never before.

Something is very wrong. Yet no one is reporting it. No one is investigating. We're not even allowed to ask questions for fear of being slandered, ostracized, or banned from social media.

This scam I'm talking about is not Covid-19. Covid is real—it's a flu pandemic. This isn't the first flu pandemic. It won't be the last. As a matter of fact, many Americans are sick again with Covid.

The strange thing is, every single person I know who is experiencing Covid again is triple-vaxxed. How's that work? If I told you everyone I met who was sick with Polio had gotten three Polio shots, would you consider the polio vaccine a success? Or a miserable failure?

This world-class scam is easy to see...

It's the response by the government, President Biden, Democrat politicians, Dr. Fauci, the CDC, and the media regarding the Covid vaccines. Something is very wrong. Something has gone very badly. We are off the rails.

And not only does no one want to talk about it, or discuss it, or debate it...

Not only is the media and social media involved in the biggest blackout, whitewash, and cover-up in history...

Our government, medical experts, and the media—all the powers that be are all still pushing this dangerous and deadly jab, despite the evidence of massive injuries and deaths. Does this make sense? Can anyone explain this?

Here is a real-life healthcare story that goes a long way to explaining it all.

One of my close friends thought he was having a heart attack. He asked me to drive him to the hospital. Of course, I dropped everything and rushed him to the ER at Summerlin Hospital in Las Vegas.

He was kept at the hospital for 22 hours. He was given a battery of tests. He passed them all with flying colors. The doctors could find nothing wrong. Thank God—there was no heart attack. He was given a clean bill of health. It must have been a "panic attack." Because he is in perfect health.

About two weeks later the bill came. 22 hours in the hospital. Not even one full day. Nothing wrong—so, no treatments of any kind were given.

The bill was $115,000.

He was in shock. The bill could have given him a real heart attack. This is insanity. The healthcare system is a scam. Thanks, Obamacare. What a great job Obama did to "fix" healthcare. Now 22 hours in a hospital costs $115,000. The frauds in the media won't dare talk about that story.

This also explains everything about the past two years of this Covid pandemic. This is why the reaction to Covid by the media, Democrat politicians and medical "experts" has been so hysterical, panicked and exaggerated. It's all about the money.

Here's a simple explanation of the world's biggest "get-rich-quick" Ponzi scheme.

First, Biden, Dr. Fauci, the CDC, FDA, Democrat politicians and the media scare people to death—for the flu with mainly mild to moderate symptoms, with a 99.9% recovery rate. Then, they whip Americans into a frenzy. This turns Americans into paranoid hypochondriacs and hospital junkies.

"If it bleeds, it leads." The more death on the front page, or at the top of the news, the more papers they sell, the higher the ratings for the TV news. And, of course, the more billions of dollars spent by Big Pharma on drug and vaccine ads as a "thank you" to the media. This frightens and panics more Americans into taking the vaccine. And the more hysteria, panic and fear, the more Americans rush to the hospital ER.

It's one big vicious cycle that makes everyone at the top filthy rich.

Think of that $115,000 bill for 22 hours in the hospital. That's for a person that wasn't sick. What if you have the flu? Once at the ER, they'll admit you for a day, or two, or three, out of caution (and fear of a lawsuit), and you'll go home with a $250,000 bill.

What if you get seriously ill? That's a trip to the ICU. Whether you live, or die, either way someone gets a $5,000,000 bill.

Multiply these bills times millions of hysterical, scared-to-death Americans who rush to the hospital ER at the first sign of a cold, cough, fever, or sneeze. Most of them are poor and on Obamacare or Medicaid. And it's all paid by OPM—other people's money. So, the government pays, and pays, and pays some more.

With your taxpayer money.

Everyone involved gets rich quickly: the hospitals, doctors, Big Pharma, ventilator makers, mask makers, Covid antigen test makers, vaccine manufacturers, the media that books billions of dollars in Big Pharma ads, and maybe most of all, the politicians.

Think how much money the hysteria, panic and fear porn, combined with vaccine mandates, have made each Democrat politician that owns stock in publicly-traded hospitals, healthcare, drug and vaccine companies?

And this is all separate from the obscene bonuses paid by the government to hospitals for each patient that tests positive for Covid; dies with Covid; or gets put on those deadly ventilators. The sicker you are, the more money everyone makes. Keep in mind, they only get paid gigantic bonuses if you're sick, or dead.

I haven't even mentioned all the Americans experiencing heart attacks, strokes, blood clots and advanced cancer directly from the Covid vaccine itself. See the VAERS list. Literally, hundreds of thousands of Americans have gotten sick, crippled, permanently disabled or died as a direct result of the Covid vaccine. That's not my opinion, it's all spelled out in the VAERS report (Vaccine Adverse Event Reporting System).

So, there's another multi-billion-dollar income stream.

And this terrible world-class scam is made possible by a conspiracy of government and media slandering and banning the only cheap, highly effective miracle drugs and vitamins that work for pennies on the dollar- like Ivermectin, HCQ (hydroxychloroquine), zinc, quercetin, and Vitamins C and D3.

Incidentally, I have on my desktop literally hundreds of studies worldwide that prove the effectiveness of these therapeutics, if taken within the first few days of Covid. They work like a miracle, according to study after study. These same therapeutics wiped out Covid almost overnight in the slums of India.

But you've never heard about any of these studies, right? That's because none of them have been featured in the mainstream media. We have experienced a total media blackout of the drugs and vitamins that work against Covid—and they happen to be inexpensive too. No coincidence.

This same media claims over one million Americans died from Covid—yet they've blacked out, whitewashed, and covered up the only therapeutics that work effectively. And to top it off, at the same time, they refuse to cover all the deaths and injuries from the product they're pushing—the vaccine—that clearly doesn't work.

Bernie Madoff is rolling over in his grave.

But here is the all-important Part II of my story. Now that we know this whole thing was overblown and exaggerated to scare you to death, and the vaccines don't work as advertised (not even close); now that we know the vaccines are dangerous and deadly; now that we know the lockdowns, mask and vaccine mandates, school closures, business closures accomplished nothing; they led to more illness, death, depression, addiction, suicide and the destruction of our economy.

Why can't anyone responsible for doing all this to us admit they were wrong?

Let me tell you another story that explains it all. Years ago, a trusted friend and employee of mine (let's call him "Phil") stole $1,000 cash from my office. I knew in every bone in my body that it was him. He was the only one near my office during the lunch break. He always went out to lunch, but not on the one day, the money went missing. He was in a desperate situation and needed the money.

Most telling of all, as Shakespeare would say, "He doth protest too much." That was the real tip-off. He was over-the-top hysterical at the mere thought of me asking him about the crime. He was crying, screaming, begging, banging the table, and pacing back and forth like a madman. He swore repeatedly he didn't do it, he swore on his mother's grave. He feigned disbelief that his friend (me) could ever accuse him of such a thing. His reaction was so over-the-top, I knew he did it. Nobody innocent would react like that.

I never trusted him again. I never treated him as a friend again. A few weeks later he left the company. We never spoke again.

Fast forward twenty-five years. Out of the blue, he called me a few years ago to confess. He said, "Remember that missing $1,000 from 25 years ago? You were right. I stole it. I was so desperate. But once I lied to you, swore I didn't do it, and acted so offended and outraged at the mere idea of you accusing me, I was in so deep, there was no going back. My lie was just too big. I had to stick to my story. I'm sorry. I've carried this burden for 25 years. I just needed to find you and call you and confess. I'm so sorry."

That explains this entire Covid response.

They're all in too deep. The lie is just too big. The results are too catastrophic. They've acted too hysterical and over-the-top. There's no going back.

It started out with greed. Everyone involved wanted to get rich quickly. They saw Covid and the vaccine as a way to get filthy rich, unimaginably rich. Rich enough for the next ten generations of their families. "FU money" as they say. And they could pay for it all with OPM—"other people's money". They'd get the government to pay the whole bill.

Many conservative media personalities throw around the term "de-population scheme" to explain what's happening with vaccines. They use the term "mass murder." And it is (in my opinion) mass murder if the medical experts in charge and Big Pharma executives knew it was deadly but pushed the jab anyway.

But everyone involved didn't want to kill off half the world's population. I do believe there were people at the very top of this scam, this pyramid scheme, who are pure evil. But most of the people involved are not "mass murderers."

Doctors don't wake up in the morning and dream of killing all their patients. ICU nurses don't arrive at work looking forward to mass murder. As much as I despise the fake news media, I don't think they're all in on mass murder.

This evil disaster was all about one thing: pure, unadulterated greed. The almighty dollar. More money to go around than anyone had ever seen in their lifetimes. Everyone's eyes got as big as saucers.

And then they drank the Kool-Aid.

They wanted to believe in the vaccines (and the masks, and the lockdowns, and the small business closures). They wanted to believe they could "do good," while getting filthy rich. They wanted to believe the vaccines worked. They wanted to believe they were saving lives. They wanted to believe they were heroes. They wanted desperately to believe anyone who called the vaccine dangerous or deadly was spreading "misinformation" and had to be stopped. So they convinced themselves they had to censor, ban, terminate anyone who disagreed, or dissented from "the company storyline".

And like my friend who stole the $1,000, once they went far down this road and sold their souls, there was no going back. They were in too deep. So, to admit it was all a lie, a deception, a fraud, a "get-rich-quick" scheme, a Bernie Madoff Ponzi scheme, means they are guilty of massive crimes against humanity. To admit they made a mistake, were wrong, were duped, or were greedy, and now regret it is to admit they misled the world, and they are complicit in millions of deaths and injuries across the globe. That's called "mass murder." It's certainly (at best) manslaughter.

It's not like they can wake up one day and say "Oops, I made a mistake. I was wrong. This was just the flu. All the lockdowns, masks, vaccines, vaccine mandates, vaccine passports, business closures, school closures, and hundred-thousand-dollar and million-dollar medical bills were all for nothing. I'm sorry. Can we have a do-over?"

Ask my friend Phil. That's not easy to do or say. Not when the issue is $1,000 theft, let alone when the issue is millions of deaths and injuries worldwide, trillions of dollars in business losses and medical expenses, millions of jobs and careers destroyed, millions of businesses closed, dreams shattered, and a society in shambles.

So instead of apologizing, the media, Democrat politicians and "medical experts" are either doubling down (claiming they were right all along and saved lives) or erasing history and moving on. They hope you forget the past two years. They hope you remember them as heroes, fighting for your health, while they damaged or destroyed your health and/or your career (or both). And never forget the damage they did to your children's lives.

But hey, be thankful. At least you're one of the lucky ones who is still alive.

Now that you know the truth, now that you've seen the light, all I ask is that you never forget; that you remember everything that happened; remember who misled you; who cost you; who bankrupted you; who made you sick, or sicker; who led to the death of your friends and family by force vaccinating them, or suppressing the truth about therapeutics that actually work; who got filthy rich off your misery.

Then hold them responsible on Election Day 2024 (and all future Election Days).

I guarantee you only one thing—if we allow the socialists, communists, fascists, tyrants, greedy globalists, and insane-with-power control freaks who did this to us to remain in office, it will start all over again, it will all come roaring back, it will never end.

We will become Australia or Austria, or China—locked up and locked down for long periods, until we close our businesses, or lose our jobs, and become poor and dependent on the government. Not just poor and locked down, but forced to wear masks permanently, and forced to take a dangerous, deadly experimental jab with the government's boot on our neck.

In all future elections, vote like your life and your children's life depends on it. Because it does.

Confronting Evil: Here's My Simple Challenge to Dr. Fauci, the CDC, FDA, Big Pharma & Democrats

There is nothing left to debate. Anyone who is not brainwashed, or brain dead, can see that the Covid vaccine was the worst mistake in America's history, world history, healthcare history and the history of medicine.

The data is in from all over the world. Haven't you seen it? That's because the media is guilty of covering up mass death on a scale no one can even imagine. But it's only getting started. Wait for 2023.

But I have all the important data. Write me. I'm glad to send it. For free: WayneRoot@gmail.com.

No, I'm not a doctor or a scientist. Yes, I'm a conservative TV and radio talk show host. But I'm not brainwashed, gaslighted, delusional, or easily scammed. I only search for raw truth—wherever it leads.

I have seen the data (i.e., factual evidence) from all over the world that the Covid vaccine is the most dangerous and deadly vaccine in history — BY A MILE.

I have seen the data that shows mortality rates are up by the most in history, far more than World War 2—and these deaths are up only since the Covid vaccines were introduced.

I have seen the data that shows mortality rates are through the roof—but only among the vaccinated and not among the unvaccinated.

I have seen the data that shows the more Covid boosters you take, the higher the death rate goes.

I have seen the data that shows the highest death rate is among Millennials aged 25 to 54 (working-age young adults forced by OSHA mandates to take the Covid vaccine).

If you're not blind, you've noticed the media headlines of "sudden death." The numbers are shocking. Every day more famous people are "dying suddenly and unexpectedly". But that's just the tip of the iceberg. They represent thousands per day dying suddenly. A phenomenon never seen in history until the vaccines.

But it's not just death. It's a pandemic of disability. It's heart attacks, myocarditis, strokes, blood clots and an explosion of Stage 4 cancer. Millions of Americans will never work again. Who will pay for all this?

This is a tsunami of death and disability—all because these innocent Americans trusted the government, Dr. Fauci, the CDC, FDA, Big Pharma and Democrat politicians who mandated the vaccines.

Big mistake. As Ronald Reagan once said, "The nine most terrifying words in the English language are: I'm from the government, and I'm here to help."

So, here's my challenge to all the liars, frauds, peddlers of propaganda, merchants of death, and kings and queens of cover-up and denial. It's simple.

I believe the Covid vaccine is deadly. This is now a crime scene. This is mass death on a grand scale. This vaccine death spiral is accelerating at warp speed. I believe we are about to experience the biggest mass die-off in world history in 2023.

So, please prove me wrong. Make me eat crow. Make me look crazy. All you have to do is take a simple lie detector test.

I ask the following suspects to take the test, Dr Fauci, CDC officials, FDA officials, Big Pharma CEOs and top Biden administration officials. Please answer these few simple questions and show us the results…Then, answer YES or NO.

1. Did you personally take the Covid vaccine?
2. Did your spouse take it?
3. Did your children take it?
4. Does it protect against Covid?
5. Does it prevent transmission?
6. Did you see the pre-trial vaccine results with large numbers of deaths, miscarriages, heart attacks and strokes?
7. Are you aware that the vaccine manufacturers wanted the pre-trial results sealed for 75 years?
8. In 1976 the entire swine flu vaccine program was suspended because 32 Americans died. Are you aware the VAERS list shows tens of thousands are dead from the Covid vaccine, more than all other vaccines in modern history COMBINED?
9. Were you aware that hundreds of studies show Hydroxychloroquine (HCQ) and Ivermectin work very effectively versus Covid and other viruses?
10. Are you aware millions of lives could have been saved with HCQ, Ivermectin and Vitamin D3? However, Big Pharma could not have admitted they were effective versus Covid because they wouldn't have gotten emergency authorization to make billions of dollars with their experimental Covid vaccines.
11. Have you or your family ever used Ivermectin?

We can clear this right up with Dr. Fauci, top medical authorities, Big Pharma and Democrat politicians answering these questions on a lie detector test. If they pass, I'm a fool, I'm wrong and you'll shut me up forever. You win, I lose. You're heroes.

So, if you have nothing to hide, take the test.

If I'm right, and the needle shows they fail every question, this makes them all complicit in fraud and mass murder. They all knew from the start. They all certainly know the truth now. Yet they're still pushing the vaccine.

You can take the lie detector test and prove me a fool. I dare you. I double dare you.

But no one will ever take me up on my challenge.

That's because the debate is over. The jig is up. They can't hide it anymore. The "sudden deaths" are piling up. Now it's all about denial and cover-up.

P.S. My favorite pronouns are "Crimes/Against/Humanity" "Mass/Murder" and "Prosecute/Fauci/And Everyone Involved"

Why This Anti-Covid Vaccine TV Host Will Always Support This Pro-Covid Vaccine President

By Wayne Allyn Root

I have more proof liberals, Democrats and assorted socialists/communists/Marxists/globalists are dead wrong. This is the greatest nation in world history, ever blessed by God. The streets are paved with gold. This is the land of opportunity. Our history isn't evil—it's better than any country, ever.

Here's the proof: my life.

I'm living the American Dream. I'm a blue-collar S.O.B.—son of a butcher. My father and mother were first-generation Americans. My father wore a bloody white apron to work and cut meat for rich people—who treated him like dirt.

Yet I recently conducted my 11th interview with the 45th President of the United States. You can watch it here:

https://rumble.com/v21ywty-in-interview-with-donal d-trump-122422.html

Not only is this my 11th interview with President Trump—perhaps as many, or more, than any TV or radio host in America. But I was honored to be chosen as the opening speaker for presidential candidate Trump and President Trump at seven events (with thousands attending) here in Las Vegas.

I was invited to the White House six times.

I am a Jewish American and I was blessed to attend the "Abraham Accords" signing ceremony at the White House between Israel and her Arab neighbors.

To top it off, my wife Cindy and I were blessed to honeymoon last spring at Mar-a-lago as guests on the estate of President Trump.

And in the past year, I became the host of not one, but two new conservative television shows on Real America's Voice TV Network and Lindell TV (yes, Mike Lindell the MyPillow man's network at FrankSpeech.com).

Only in America. God bless America.

Now to my interview with #45 (and I hope #47, too). Because we are friends and enjoy mutual respect, President Trump and I always have unique and often ground-breaking interviews.

Trump joined me for the second time on my Real America's Voice TV show, "America's Top Ten Countdown," on Christmas Eve 2022. I brought up several controversial topics—his relationship with the Jewish people; his infamous Kanye West dinner; his support of backstabber Kevin McCarthy; his opinion of GOP traitor Mitch McConnell and the obscene $1.7 trillion-dollar omnibus spending bill passed in late December 2022; and drumroll, please…

The Covid vaccine controversy.

That's the big one and the point of this chapter. Millions of conservatives who follow me on TV, radio, in newspaper columns, books, and social media (I'm back on Twitter again @RealWayneRoot), know me as "the Paul Revere" of the Covid vaccine. This is because I've warned louder and with more passion, from the highest mountaintops, about the dangerous, deadly Covid jab—literally from the first day.

This vaccine is the biggest disaster in healthcare history. It's a complete failure. It doesn't prevent Covid. It doesn't prevent the spread of Covid. And I have data and hard evidence from around the world showing the deaths, injuries, heart attacks, strokes, and massive immune damage these vaccines have produced. The mortality rate is skyrocketing across America and worldwide to the highest levels in recorded history—but only since the introduction of the Covid jab and among the vaccinated.

But President Trump disagrees. He thinks the vaccines are a miracle of modern science. He believes they saved millions of lives.

Two people couldn't be farther apart.

So how can I support Trump for president? Well, I don't just support Trump, I support him 110%. I'm "all in" with Trump, even though we disagree on the Covid vaccine. Why?

First, we agree 100% on virtually every other issue. That puts us on the same team. I always look at the glass as half full!

Second, above all else, I'm a businessman, CEO, entrepreneur, and capitalist evangelist. Business will always be number one for me. It's in my body and soul. Trump was the greatest economic president of my lifetime, maybe ever. His economy was close to perfection—Trump produced great prosperity; historic middle-class income growth; the lowest unemployment ever; low taxes; low regulations; skyrocketing stock market; exploding real estate; along with no inflation and low-interest rates.

We need Trump back. Now. Today. We need the Trump economic miracle back.

Now to the Covid vaccine controversy. Watch my interview with President Trump (link above). What matters, above all else, is that Trump is against any Covid vaccine mandate. Trump will never force anyone to take the jab. Period.

No cop will ever have to take the jab; no fireman; no nurse; no private sector employee; no government employee; no pilot; no soldier. NO ONE.

Bravo!

Trump also promised to reinstate any military member who was fired for refusing to take the jab—and give them back all their back pay.

Even bigger bravo!

And then there's the children. With Trump as president no child will ever be forced to take the jab to attend public school, or college. When it comes to children, Trump went further. He said, "Children shouldn't have them. They don't need them. It's terrible what they've done to children."

Triple bravo!

That's all I need to hear. It's a free country. Trump can love the vaccine; I can hate it. But, if no one is forced to take it, it doesn't matter.

If you want it, get it. Good luck. You'll need it. But I will never get it. I will encourage all my family, friends, and fans to run away from it. That's freedom. That's what America is all about.

That's why I'll always be in Trump's corner. He has my full support and confidence for president in 2024. We need Trump now, more than ever. MAGA.

"We must act, now. We must save freedom here. I am an immigrant. When my country succumbed to tyranny, I had somewhere to go to. If we lose freedom here, we will have nowhere to go to."

Nicky Billou

The Global Fight For Freedom

T he next couple of chapters remind us that this fight for freedom isn't just happening in America; it's happening worldwide. We are in a new version of the Cold War, and only unlike the last one, the enemy isn't as obvious to us. It's Communist China, Putin's Russia, North Korea, and the mullahs in Iran. But it's also the globalist elites of the World Economic Forum and their allies in many countries. While we can't necessarily fight the fight in each country, we can make common cause and support the brave men and women in each country that are taking on the fight.

Natan Sharansky, the brave Soviet dissident and later Israeli politician, recounted how he and the other political prisoners in the Soviet gulags would take courage and heart from passing on and reading the speeches of Ronald Reagan. He said that Reagan's famed "**Evil Empire**" speech, where he spoke about the Soviet Union as an Evil Empire that was the locus of evil in the modern world, electrified the prisoners and gave them the courage to keep resisting their captors and standing for freedom.

The "**Evil Empire**" speech was delivered by Ronald Reagan to the National Association of Evangelicals on March 8, 1983, during the height of the Cold War. In that speech, Reagan referred to the Soviet Union as an "evil empire" and as "the locus of evil in the modern world". Reagan explicitly rejected the notion that the United States and the Soviet Union were equally responsible for the Cold War and the ongoing nuclear arms race between the two nations; rather, he asserted that the conflict was a battle between good and evil.

Here is an excerpt from this great speech. Go watch it on Rumble or YouTube.

"Yes, let us pray for the salvation of all of those who live in that totalitarian darkness—pray they will discover the joy of knowing God. But until they do, let us be aware that while they preach the supremacy of the State, declare its omnipotence over individual man, and predict its eventual domination of all peoples on the earth, they are the locus of evil in the modern world... So, in your discussions of the nuclear freeze proposals, I urge you to beware the temptation of pride—the temptation of blithely declaring yourselves above it all and label both sides equally at fault, to ignore the facts of history and the aggressive impulses of an evil empire, to simply call the arms race a giant misunderstanding and thereby remove yourself from the struggle between right and wrong and good and evil."

America:
The Indispensable
Nation

By Nicky Billou

W e are living in perilous times. The forces of globalism are pushing hard to extinguish freedom all around the globe. The Covid lockdowns and vaccine mandates were a global phenomenon. Many formerly free countries used this manufactured crisis to unprecedentedly take away people's freedoms.

My own home country of Canada was one of the most egregious offenders, where the Premiers of virtually every province and the Prime Minister of Canada imposed mask mandates, vaccine mandates, and government-imposed restrictions on travel and business activity. The governments of New Zealand, Australia, the UK, and most of the EU followed suit.

While there has been pushback domestically against some of these policies, and most of them have been overturned, the threat of other manufactured crises is very real. The globalist government of the Netherlands is attempting to force its farmers to give up farming on 30% of their farming land to satisfy the false green narrative that farms contribute to "climate change". Justin Trudeau has been attempting to do the same thing in Canada. The Chinese Communist government has been imposing horrific zero Covid policies, locking people up in their homes and offices and not allowing them to leave!

America's moral authority as a symbol of freedom is one of the things that has given brave men and women worldwide hope and optimism for the future. Great Americans have always stood up and inspired freedom lovers around the world with their words and their actions.

Thomas Jefferson did it first, with the ringing words of the Declaration Of Independence *"We hold these truths to be self-evident, That all men are created equal, That they are endowed by their creator with certain inalienable rights, That among these are Life, Liberty, and The Pursuit Of Happiness, And that to secure these rights, Governments are constituted among men that derive their just powers from the consent of the governed"*.

Lincoln did it with his brilliant stand for human freedom in the Emancipation Proclamation "I, Abraham Lincoln, President of the United States, by virtue of the power in me vested as Commander-in-Chief, of the Army and Navy of the United States in time of actual armed rebellion against authority and government of the United States, and as a fit and necessary war measure for suppressing said rebellion, do... order and designate as the States and parts of States wherein the people thereof respectively, are this day in rebellion, against the United States, the following, to wit:"

"I do order and declare that all persons held as slaves within said designated States, and parts of States, are, and henceforward shall be free... [S]uch persons of suitable condition, will be received into the armed service of the United States... And upon this act, sincerely believed to be an act of justice, warranted by the Constitution, upon military necessity, I *invoke the considerate judgment of mankind and the gracious favor of Almighty God...."* *(emphasis added)*

And his immortal Gettysburg Address:

"Four score and seven years ago our fathers brought forth on this continent, a new nation, conceived in Liberty, and dedicated to the proposition that all men are created equal.

Now we are engaged in a great civil war, testing whether that nation or any nation so conceived and dedicated can long endure. We are met on a great battlefield of that war. We have come to dedicate a portion of that field, as a final resting place for those who here gave their lives that that nation might live. It is altogether fitting and proper that we should do this.

But, in a larger sense, we cannot dedicate—we cannot consecrate—we cannot hallow—this ground. The brave men, living and dead, who struggled here, have consecrated it, far above our poor power to add or detract. The world will little note, nor long remember what we say here, but it can never forget what they did here. It is for us the living, rather, to be dedicated here to the unfinished work which they who fought here have thus far so nobly advanced. It is rather for us to be here dedicated to the great task remaining before us—that from these honored dead we take increased devotion to that cause for which they gave the last full measure of devotion—that we here highly resolve that these dead shall not have died in vain—that this nation, under God, shall have a new birth of freedom—and *that government of the people, by the people, for the people, shall not perish from the earth." (emphasis added)*

John F. Kennedy did it with these immortal lines from his Inaugural Address "We shall pay any price, bear any burden, meet any hardship, support any friend, oppose any foe to assure the survival and success of liberty".

Martin Luther King did it with this soaring rhetoric in his I Have A Dream Speech: "This will be the day when all of God's children will be able to sing with new meaning "My country 'tis of thee, sweet land of liberty, of thee I sing. Land where my father's died, land of the Pilgrim's pride, from every mountainside, let freedom ring!"

And if America is to be a great nation, this must become true. So let freedom ring from the hilltops of New Hampshire. Let freedom ring from the mighty mountains of New York.

Let freedom ring from the heightening Alleghenies of Pennsylvania.

Let freedom ring from the snow-capped Rockies of Colorado.

Let freedom ring from the curvaceous slopes of California.

But not only that, let freedom, ring from Stone Mountain of Georgia.

Let freedom ring from every hill and molehill of Mississippi and every mountainside.

When we let freedom ring, when we let it ring from every tenement and every hamlet, from every state and every city, we will be able to speed up that day when all of God's children, black men and white men, Jews and Gentiles, Protestants and Catholics, will be able to join hands and sing in the words of the old spiritual, *"Free at last, free at last. Thank God Almighty, we are free at last." (emphasis added)*

And Reagan did it in too many speeches to count, but these inspiring lines from his famous Tear Down This Wall Speech given at the Berlin Wall: "We welcome change and openness; for we believe that freedom and security go together, that the advance of human liberty can only strengthen the cause of world peace. There is one sign the Soviets can make that would be unmistakable, that would advance dramatically the cause of freedom and peace. General Secretary Gorbachev, if you seek peace, if you seek prosperity for the Soviet Union and Eastern Europe, if you seek liberalization: Come here to this gate! Mr. Gorbachev, open this gate! *Mr. Gorbachev, tear down this wall!" (emphasis added)*

America and Americans have always stood for freedom, not just here in America, but around the world. Twice in the last century, the so-called civilized nations of Europe dragged the world into war that destroyed the lives of tens of millions of people, and who had to come and save them, but the cornhuskers from Iowa and Nebraska, the cotton pickers from Alabama and Georgia, the steelworkers from Pennsylvania and Ohio, the auto workers from Michigan, and the surfers from California. Where would Europe—indeed the world—be without the United States today? Under the Nazi jackboot or the Soviet hammer and sickle.

And the world still needs America. Not to go and fight its wars, but to take a stand for freedom and give hope to freedom lovers everywhere. President Trump did that while keeping America out of needless wars. Let's make sure that the MAGA movement always stands for freedom everywhere, in the best tradition of America's greatest leaders and heroes.

CHAPTER 31

Truckers, Farmers, & Teenage Girls: The Unlikely Champions Of Freedom

By Nicky Billou

I n 2022, an unlikely group of men and women stood up globally to shake off the tyrants' yoke, and demand freedom for themselves and their people. These men and women deserve to be recognized and to have your admiration and support.

American patriots have always recognized like-minded patriots in other countries. In 2022, the Canadian Truckers stood up for freedom and against the tyrannical vaccine mandates implemented by the fascistic Trudeau government. They organized a convoy that started on

Canada's West Coast and drove east to Ottawa. There, they organized a very peaceful protest, requesting to meet with the Prime Minister and discuss their grievances, namely against the vaccine mandates. One of the organizers, Pat King, was interviewed on Nicky's podcast and spoke passionately and powerfully about the Trucker's goals, which were to have the illegal and fascistic vaccine mandates repealed. His argument was common sensical, namely that Truckers drove alone and were in their truck cabs, so they were not really a transmission risk to anyone, and the vaccine mandates made no sense. (This was before it became clear that the so-called vaccine didn't prevent anyone from catching Covid.)

Trudeau refused to meet them. He viciously smeared them and called them white supremacists, racists and sexists. This was a particularly odd and dishonest attack, as the Trucking business in Canada is dominated by brown-skinned men, namely Punjabi Sikhs. He invoked the Emergencies Act, a wartime measure designed to be used against Canada's enemies and used it on his own citizens. He unleashed the police with horses to trample a grandmother with a walker who was protesting the vaccine mandates. He used the measure to seize citizens' bank accounts, targeting the people who had donated money to the Truckers. Thankfully, the Canadian Senate, the majority of whom were members he had appointed, balked at his invocation of the Act and signaled they would vote it down. He had not banked on them not being fascists and being actual liberals who were appalled at his actions! He was forced to withdraw his invocation of the act, and soon, all of Canada's provinces revoked their vaccine and mask mandates.

The Truckers paid a heavy price, as many of them were jailed without bail and had their free speech rights suspended. But their courage helped end the tyranny of Canadian governments at all levels, and for this, we salute them. WAR and President Trump both stood with Truckers; for this, the freedom loving people of Canada and I are forever grateful.

The Dutch Farmers began their own protest against their government, which is full of WEF-aligned globalists. Dutch farmers' organizations have launched many protests in the Netherlands, in response to the government's mediator, who has called for the forceable relocation of farming families and the seizure of up to 600 farms deemed to be the heaviest nitrogen emitters.

Farmers Defense Force leader Mark Van den Oever announced this week that Dutch farmers would once again take to the streets after the government expressed its intentions to adopt the plan presented by former deputy prime minister Johan Remkes to meet the nitrogen standards demanded by the European Union.

In 2022, globalist Dutch Prime Minister Mark Rutte announced his intentions to cut nitrogen emissions from livestock farms in half by the year 2030 to satisfy goals laid out in the European Union's Natura 2000 scheme, which requires that all EU member-states remove industry or farming from areas deemed to be of ecological importance.

For this, the Dutch Farmers are using roadblocks, protests, and other actions to force the government to back down. They are paying a heavy price, but as Holland is the world's second-largest exporter of agricultural products, this fight affects people around the world, because, without Dutch agriculture, widespread global hunger is likely to result.

American patriots should be aware of the brave stand for freedom taken by the Dutch farmers and support them in their fight against the globalists, not just on philosophical grounds, but on practical ones.

Earlier in 2022, a 22-year-old young woman in Iran, Mahsa Amini, was arrested and *beaten to death* for the "crime" of being outdoors with her head partially uncovered. This led to widespread protests all over Iran, led mainly by teenage girls and young women in their early twenties, demanding freedom, and regime change. The regime created furious crackdowns, killing over 500 protesters outright, and arresting 15,000 of them, and they have executed a few dozen so far.

These protests have captured the imagination of people around the globe. The Iranian diaspora organized protests in countries and cities all over the world. The Conservative Leader of the Opposition in Canada, Pierre Polievre, addressed the crowd at a protest in Ottawa and outlined the hard line he would take against the Iranian regime if he were elected Prime Minister. The Iranian National Men's Soccer Team spoke out for the people of Iran, and bravely refused to sing the Islamic regime's national anthem at the World Cup. This was an act of real courage, that resulted in a crackdown by the regime, including rumored threats of reprisals against their families by the security forces. (This is in stark contrast to the faux courage of American athletes, in particular LeBron James, who pretends to speak truth to power, when he actually speaks lies and carries forward the narrative of the elite and the Democrat Party, with ZERO risk to himself or his life, and with an actual reward for the false accusations he has made against people like Darryl Morey for standing up for the people of Hong Kong, and the police officer who saved the life of a teenage girl by shooting to death an armed attacker who was trying to stab her with a knife.)

I have been on several TV shows, including Wayne's, to discuss this issue and raise awareness and support amongst the American people. Rebel News in Canada did many stories on this issue, as did Bill O'Reilly on his podcast. Unfortunately, to his and his party's eternal shame, Joe Biden has been a pusillanimous non-leader on this issue. But conservatives across America and the world have joined me in bringing awareness to this issue and standing up for the brave men and women of Iran and their fight for freedom.

It has been incredible to see teenage girls show courage in going out unarmed in the street against the heavily armed thugs of the regime and face death to make their voices heard. Likewise, it has been heartening to see Iranian celebrities and athletes put their careers and lives on the line to stand up against a regime that is killing its own people. Americans need to know what is happening in Iran, and who these brave men and women are, and to elect leaders who will support them against a regime that is part of the Axis of Evil.

America has always supported freedom lovers around the world. Americans have always spoken out against evil regimes. So, let's make sure we keep doing this, always and keep standing for a world that one day has all men and women breathe free.

"We will make America Strong again. We will make America Safe again. And we will make America Great again, greater than ever before."

Donald Trump

The List

We are going to get right to the list. We are going to break it up into multiple chapters of 10-12 companies each. The first chapter is going to include the Freedom's Heroes, the 20 most patriotic American companies doing business in the marketplace today. These are companies that score at least a 4 out of 5 on each of the 6 elements of the Freedom Scale.

These companies make great products and believe in America and all that she stands for. Buy from them and get your friends and family to buy from them, too.

Freedom's Heroes: The Most Patriotic Companies In America

These are Freedom's Heroes, the 20 most patriotic American companies doing business in the marketplace today. These are companies that score at least a 4 out of 5 on each of the 6 elements of the Freedom Scale. We are very proud of these companies, and do business with all of them whenever we can.

These companies make great products and believe in America and all that she stands for. Buy from them and get your friends and family to buy from them, too. Spread the word!

1. The Trump Organization

The Trump Organization is one of the most iconic and successful companies in the world. Now run by the President's two eldest sons, Don Jr., and Eric, it is still a powerhouse in the world of Golf Course development, Hotels and Resorts, branded products and many more industries! They offer hotels, condos, and consumer products, and you should buy as much as you can from them!

To buy all the amazing merchandise offered by The Trump Organization, visit **TrumpStore.com**. They offer books, apparel, spa and kitchen stuff, drinkware and glassware, bath and body, accessories and gifts, golf merchandise, luggage, and accessories, and so much more!

They are now doing business with Liv, the new competitor to the PGA, and God bless them for bringing competition to the world of golf!

If you are a conservative, you should be staying at Trump properties, and buying merchandise and gear from the Trump Organization!

Company Name	The Trump Organization
CEO	Donald Trump Jr. & Eric Trump
Twitter Handle	@Trump
Instagram Handle	@Trump
Facebook Handle	@Trump
LinkedIn Handle	N/A
YouTube Channel	N/A
Website	**TrumpStore.com**
Industry	Real Estate, Hotels, Product Endorsement, Golf
What Makes Them Conservative	Donald Trump's Company!!

2. TRUTH Social

Truth Social became the Apple app store's #1 downloaded app, and it is THE platform for President Trump to communicate with all his followers on social media. Truth Social was created because Twitter, under their former ownership, banned President Trump, and he realized that Big Tech was out to destroy conservative speech. He and one his biggest allies, former Congressman Devin Nunes, put together an amazing team that created a free speech-based competitor to Twitter.

"TRUTH Social is America's "Big Tent" social media platform that encourages an open, free, and honest global conversation without discriminating against political ideology." That is a direct quote from the company website, and it encapsulates exactly why Truth Social deserves your support!

Company Name	Truth Social
CEO	Devin Nunes
TruthSocial Handle	@TruthSocial
Instagram Handle	N/A
Facebook Handle	N/A
LinkedIn Handle	N/A
YouTube Channel	N/A
Website	TruthSocial.com
Industry	Social Networking
What Makes Them Conservative	Donald Trump's Social Media App! Supports free-speech and Conservatism

3. MyPillow

Mike Lindell and his company MyPillow have been stalwart in the battle for freedom. It cost him plenty when his support for President Trump caused 20+ retailers to drop MyPillow. He was targeted by the FBI for no other reason than the fact that he is a Trump supporter. His company makes amazing products, they share our values, and they deserve your support. We both own MyPillow bed sheets, pillows, and towels. The bed sheets are the best we have ever had, the towels are absorbent, and the pillows are simply amazing!

Co-Author Wayne Allyn Root has a special gift for you... Just use promo code WAR to get up to 66% off every product at **MyPillow.com**.

Company Name	MyPillow
CEO	**Mike Lindell**
Twitter Handle	Proudly Suspended by Twitter
Instagram Handle	@mypillow
Facebook Handle	@MyPillow
LinkedIn Handle	/company/mypillow-inc/
YouTube Channel	MyPillow
Website	**www.mypillow.com**
Industry	Pillow Company
What Makes Them Conservative	One of Trump's biggest supporters, against Voter Fraud

4. GreatPatriotStore.com

The GreatPatriotStore.com is an online store that sells all the household products you're already using and buying—but at a fraction of the cost. And every product they offer is made in America. The company is owned by conservative patriots. And they advertise on conservative media. It's time to teach a lesson to corporate America – if companies go woke, we will make them go broke. We are so excited to tell you about GreatPatriotStore.com!

This is the answer to inflation…hundreds of the household products you are already buying…but much better quality…at far lower prices… and ALL made in the USA…by a company run by conservatives and patriots. We love shopping here!… GreatPatriotStore.com.

Plus, you'll save time and money on gas, not having to drive to the store. You buy direct from their manufacturing site and your order is shipped to your doorstep.

Just like a Costco or Sam's Club, you need to become a member. So go to GreatPatriotStore.com – fill out the form – and someone will contact you and make it really easy for you to sign up. Get better, healthier, greener, made-in-America products, from an All-American company, delivered to your front door, at a greatly reduced price.

Company Name	Great Patriot Store
CEO	Andrew Paul
Twitter Handle	N/A
Instagram Handle	N/A
Facebook Handle	N/A
LinkedIn Handle	N/A
YouTube Channel	N/A
Website	GreatPatriotStore.com
Industry	Online Retail Store
What Makes Them Conservative	They serve conservatives and patriots!

5. In-N-Out

In-N-Out Burger is a California-based institution, and they make amazing burgers, fries and milkshakes. They have also been quietly, but steadfastly conservative. The CEO pushed back against the tyrannical edicts of Governor Gavin Newsom, M(arxist)-California, stating that they did not see it as their role to be the enforcer of the state's unconstitutional vaccine mandate. They have Bible verses on their food packaging and have not adopted any woke policies. If you live in California, Nevada, Utah, Texas, Oregon, or Colorado, you should abandon the woke fast food restaurants and eat here!

Company Name	In-N-Out Burger
CEO	Lynsi Snyder-Ellingson
Twitter Handle	@innoutburger
Instagram Handle	@innout
Facebook Handle	@innout
LinkedIn Handle	/company/in-n-out-burger/
YouTube Channel	N/A
Website	**in-n-out.com**
Industry	Restaurants
What Makes Them Conservative	Supports Christian values; Has bible verses on their packaging; California locations refused to become "vaccine police."

6. Hobby Lobby

Hobby Lobby is a crafts store chain, founded and run by the conservative, Christian Green family. They famously sued the Obama Administration over the right to not fund abortions and are unabashedly patriotic. David Green, the founder, has never apologized for his beliefs and continues to support conservative and Christian values and causes.

Company Name	Hobby Lobby
CEO	David Green
Twitter Handle	@HobbyLobby
Instagram Handle	@hobbylobby
Facebook Handle	@HobbyLobby
LinkedIn Handle	/company/hobby-lobby/
YouTube Channel	Hobby Lobby
Website	**HobbyLobby.com**
Industry	Retail Company
What Makes Them Conservative	The Company that fought for the right to not pay for abortions, owned by unabashed Christians.

7. GETTR

GETTR is a brand new social media platform dedicated to free speech and giving a voice to those in society that have been censored by Big Tech. Their website says that GETTR was "founded on the principles of free speech, independent thought and rejecting political censorship and "cancel culture". With best-in-class technology, our goal is to create a marketplace of ideas in order to share freedom and democracy around the world."

GETTR was founded by Trump ally Jason Miller and is a great company that is a place where people don't get cancelled! They deserve your support.

Company Name	GETTR
CEO	Jason Miller
Twitter Handle	@GETTRofficial
Instagram Handle	@GETTRofficial
Facebook Handle	@GETTRofficial
LinkedIn Handle	Company/gettroffcial
YouTube Channel	@gettrofficial3054
Industry	Social Media Company
What Makes Them Conservative	Support free speech and against cancel culture

8.   Real America's Voice TV Network

Real America's Voice TV Network is a conservative TV network that has a full day of conservative TV programming 24/7. Its constellation of star conservative hosts like Steve Bannon, Ted Nugent, Ed Henry (formerly Fox News White House correspondent), Charlie Kirk and of course, some guy named WAR. The co-author of this book, Wayne Allyn Root has become a big star on Real America's Voice with "America's Top Ten Countdown." Gotta give a shout-out to RAV TV. Watch on Channel 219 on Dish, or RealAmericasVoice.com, or AmericasVoice app, Roku, or Pluto, and many other platforms.

Company Name	Real America's Voice TV Network
CEO	Robert J. Sigg
Twitter Handle	@RealAmVoice
Instagram Handle	@realamericasvoice
Facebook Handle	@RealAmericasVoice
LinkedIn Handle	company/realamericasvoice/
YouTube Channel	RealAmericasVoice
Website	**AmericasVoice.news**
Industry	TV Network
What Makes Them Conservative	They are THE conservative TV Network in the USA!

9. Bass Pro Shops

Bass Pro Shops is an iconic sporting goods company, and their products and services are incredible. They offer knives, guns, camping gear, boats, boating gear, apparel and so much more. Their stores are replete with pro-American slogans and imagery.

Nicky bought t-shirts made by gun manufacturers, and door mats with pro-2nd Amendment slogans just to watch liberal heads explode!

If you are an outdoorsman, Bass Pro Shops, and their sister brand, Cabela's, are where you want to do all your shopping.

Company Name	Bass Pro Shops
CEO	Johnny Morris
Twitter Handle	@BassProShops
Instagram Handle	@bassproshops
Facebook Handle	@bassproshops
LinkedIn Handle	/company/bassproshops/
YouTube Channel	Bass Pro Shops
Website	**BassPro.com**
Industry	Retail
What Makes Them Conservative	Owned by a lifelong Republican and devout Christian. Donates thousands to Republican candidates

10. Chick-Fil-A

Founded by devout Southern Baptist Truett Cathy, Chick-Fil-A has been a conservative mainstay organization.

Their corporate purpose is: "To glorify God by being a faithful steward of all that is entrusted to us and to have a positive influence on all who come in contact with Chick-fil-A."

Their food is delicious, and they are a company that, on the whole, lives their values. They deserve your support!

Company Name	**Chick-fil-A**
CEO	Andrew Truett Cathy
Twitter Handle	@ChickfilA
Instagram Handle	@chickfila
Facebook Handle	@ChickfilA
LinkedIn Handle	/company/chick-fil-a/
YouTube Channel	Chickfila
Website	**Chick-fil-A.com**
Industry	Restauraunt Chain
What Makes Them Conservative	Distributed shirts supporting the pro-law enforcement organization Blue Lives Matter; contributes to conservative and Christian causes

11. **Rumble**

Rumble is a competitor to YouTube that is immune to cancel culture. Many top conservatives have abandoned YouTube for Rumble, including Devin Nunes, Dinesh D'Souza, Dan Bongino, Sean Hannity, and Representative Jim Jordan. President Donald Trump officially joined Rumble on June 26, 2021

As of August 15, 2022, Rumble has 44 million monthly active users (MAU). Several content creators have gained a receptive audience on Rumble after their productions have been pulled from YouTube or Facebook, including Del Bigtree, Sherri Tenpenny, and Simone Gold.

In August 2021, Rumble announced deals with former Democratic Representative Tulsi Gabbard and The Intercept founder Glenn Greenwald to start posting their videos to the site. After being banned from most other platforms for being a man, boxer and social media personality Andrew Tate began posting on Rumble in August 2022. Tate's move coincided with a significant increase in downloads of the Rumble app.

DUMP YouTube! Join Rumble!!!

Company Name	Rumble
CEO	Chris Pavlovski
Twitter Handle	@ChrisPavlovski
Instagram Handle	N/A
Facebook Handle	N/A
LinkedIn Handle	company/rumble-com
YouTube Channel	N/A
Website	**rumble.com**
Industry	Competitor to YouTube
What Makes Them Conservative	Free Speech Social Media Platform

12. Goya Foods

Goya Foods is a $1.5 billion food company owned by the Unane family. The CEO, Robert Unane, has been a vocal Trump supporter, and his support of President Trump led the Marxist Congresswoman Sandy Cortez of New York to call for a boycott.

Thankfully, patriotic Americans bought more Goya products than ever, and despite the lack of support of some members of the family, Robert Unane has stuck to his guns and continued to support the President.

They are a company that cares and values true diversity, not the fake kind the Left uses as a cudgel to silence dissent. La Gran Familia Goya is one that operates like a family that loves and cares about all involved in their activities.

Goya makes great food products, and they deserve your support!

Company Name	Goya Foods
CEO	Robert Unane
Twitter Handle	@GoyaFoods
Instagram Handle	@GoyaFoods
Facebook Handle	@GoyaFoods
LinkedIn Handle	/company/goya-foods
YouTube Channel	Goya Foods
Website	**goya.com**
Industry	Latino Foods
What Makes Them Conservative	The CEO basically told the woke to take a hike

13. Interstate Batteries

Interstate Battery System of America, Inc., a.k.a. Interstate Batteries, is a privately-owned battery marketing and distribution company. It markets automotive batteries manufactured by Brookfield Business Partners, Exide Technologies, and others through independent distributors.

The company is headquartered in Dallas, Texas, and it also markets marine/RV, mobility, motorcycle, lawn and garden, and other lines of batteries in the starting, lighting and ignition (SLI) markets. Interstate Batteries operates a distributor network that supplies batteries to over 200,000 dealers. They also have distributors in Bermuda, Bolivia, Canada, Costa Rica, the Dominican Republic, Guatemala, Guyana, Haiti, Honduras, Nicaragua and Panama. Additionally, they operate over 200 corporate and franchise owned retail stores.

They are led by a staunch Christian, Scott Miller. Here is an excerpt from their website:

"What Makes Us Inherently Us

Interstate Batteries® is a mission-driven company fueled by our Purpose (to glorify God) and guided by our Values:

- Love
- Servant's Heart
- Excellence
- Courage
- Community
- Joy
- Integrity

Interstate team members can expect a flexible work environment respectful of life-work balance that also offers opportunity to play a role in the transformation of a decades-old iconic brand.

Our engagement surveys tell us that Interstate team members value working for a company with a purpose greater than just making money or selling batteries. Team members appreciate being able to bring their whole selves to a workplace that seeks to nourish not only their professional, but also their physical, emotional and spiritual health. The ability to work on progressive, innovative and often industry-changing projects also rates very highly on our surveys."

"Our Purpose

To glorify God and enrich lives as we deliver the most trustworthy source of power to the world.

We fulfill our purpose by doing business based on biblical principles – such as honesty, humility, service and care – in a way that is welcoming and loving to all. As a company contributor, you are free to interact with the purpose in whatever way is most meaningful to you. Our values, however, are unchanging, and we ask that our team members try their best to live them as they serve our key stakeholders: team members, customers, distributors and franchisees, suppliers and vendors, communities and shareholders. By creating a welcoming and caring environment, we hope to create a positive experience for our team members and everyone else whom Interstate touches, no matter their background or belief system."

These guys deserve your support!!

Company Name	Interstate Batteries
CEO	Scott Miller
Twitter Handle	@interstatebatts
Instagram Handle	@interstatebatteries
Facebook Handle	@InsterstateBatteries
LinkedIn Handle	/company/interstate-batteries/
YouTube Channel	Interstate Batteries
Website	**InterstateBatteries.com**
Industry	Consumer Goods
What Makes Them Conservative	Led by outspoken Christian, invests company money into promoting God's love in mainstream television advertisements

14. The Epoch Times

The Epoch Times is a freedom-based international multi-language newspaper and media company affiliated with the Falun Gong new religious movement. The Epoch Times is the fastest-growing independent news media in North America. It is nonpartisan and dedicated to truthful reporting.

The Epoch Times was founded in North America in the year 2000 in response to communist repression and censorship in China. Its founders are Chinese immigrants who themselves had fled communism and have sought to create an independent media to bring the world uncensored and truthful information.

The newspaper, based in New York City, is part of the Epoch Media Group, which also operates New Tang Dynasty (NTD) Television. The Epoch Times has operated in 21 languages in 33 countries.

The Epoch Times opposes the Chinese Communist Party, promotes freedom-minded politicians in Europe, and has championed the GOAT himself, former President Donald Trump in the U.S.

The Epoch Times is free from the influence of any government, corporation, or political party—this is what makes them different from other media organizations. Here is a quote for their website that should apply to every media organization:

"Our goal is to bring our readers accurate information so they can form their own opinions about the most significant topics of our time.

We don't follow the unhealthy trend of agenda-driven journalism prevalent in today's media environment.

Instead, we use our principles of Truth and Tradition as our guiding light. We highlight in our reporting the best of humanity, the valuable lessons of history, and traditions that are beneficial for society."

Company Name	The Epoch Times
CEO	John Tang
Twitter Handle	@EpochTimes
Instagram Handle	@EpochTimes
Facebook Handle	@EpochTimes
LinkedIn Handle	/company/the-epoch-times/
YouTube Channel	The Epoch Times
Website	**TheEpochTimes.com**
Industry	Media
What Makes Them Conservative	Holds "Truth and Tradition" as tagline and principles.

15. UFC

The UFC, under the leadership of Dana White, has become the last bastion of traditional America-loving sports and athletics. Dana is a close, personal friend of President Trump's, and spoke at the Republican National Convention in both 2016 and 2020, enthusiastically and cogently supporting President Trump. White is the toughest CEO in America, and many UFC stars are openly pro-Trump and anti-Communist, especially Colby Covington, Jorge Masvidal, Rose Namajunas, and Beneil Dariush.

If you love America and sports, you've got to support the UFC! Buy their pay-per-views, go to their live events, and buy a piece of the UFC by investing in their parent company, Endeavor's, stock.

Company Name	UFC
CEO	Dana White
Twitter Handle	@UFC
Instagram Handle	@UFC
Facebook Handle	@UFC
LinkedIn Handle	/company/UFC
YouTube Channel	UFC
Website	**UFC.com**
Stock Symbol	**EDR (NYSE)**
Industry	Combat Sports
What Makes Them Conservative	Dana White is a personal friend of Donald Trump. White spoke at the 2016 & 2020 Republican National Conventions

16. Point Bridge Capital

Point Bridge Capital has created a MAGA fund that invests in firms supporting GOP values, massively outperforming the woke ESG funds in which the Biden administration wants 401(k)s to invest in.

Point Bridge Capital, which goes by the ticker MAGA, was doing 15 percent better than ESG Funds and 13 percent better than the S&P 500 this year, according to a Bloomberg analysis.

The company, which holds $1.45 billion in assets, stands on the opposite end of the political spectrum to ESG funds, which focus investments on environmental, social and corporate governance principles.

Their two criteria for investing in a firm are that the majority of a company's political donations need to go to the Republican party, and the majority of their assets and business need to be in the USA.

If you invest in securities and want to put your investment dollars in companies supporting your values, you can buy the MAGA ETF!

Company Name	MAGA Fund
CEO	Hal Lambert
Twitter Handle	N/A
Instagram Handle	N/A
Facebook Handle	@PointBridgeCapital
LinkedIn Handle	company/pointbridge1
YouTube Channel	N/A
Website	**PointBridgeCapital.com**
ETF Ticker	MAGA
Industry	Investment Company
What Makes Them Conservative	Invests In Companies with Republican values

17. LL Bean

L.L.Bean is a privately held retail company founded in 1912 by Leon Leonwood Bean. They headquartered the company where it was founded, in Freeport, Maine. It specializes in clothing and outdoor recreation equipment. It has over $1.6 Billion annual revenues and more than 6400 employees.

Linda Bean, one of the descendants of founder Leon Leonwood Bean, who sits on the board of directors, donated US $60,000 to a political action committee that supported Donald Trump's 2016 presidential campaign. Trump posted on Twitter, in support of Linda Bean after calls for the boycott, "Thank you to Linda Bean of L.L. Bean for your great support and courage. People will support you even more now. Buy L.L. Bean."

LL Bean's website is free of the wokist garbage and sticks to business and serving its customers.

Company Name	L.L. Bean
CEO	Stephen Smith
Twitter Handle	@LLBean
Instagram Handle	@LLBean
Facebook Handle	@LLBean
LinkedIn Handle	/company/llbean/
YouTube Channel	L.L.Bean
Website	**llbean.com**
Industry	Retail Company
What Makes Them Conservative	Contributed to the Trump Presidential Campaign, supports Conservative causes

18. Emerson Knives

Ernest Emerson founded Emerson Knives in 1979 in California. He invented the tactical folding knife for the Navy SEALS, and his company has been making knives, coffee, gear and apparel in the good ole US of A. They make amazing knives and their apparel is well-designed and well made. Ernie and his team are all patriots, and their stuff is amazing.

We highly recommend that you buy all their stuff. It's awesome, and you are supporting an America-loving company.

Company Name	Emerson Knives
CEO	Ernest Emerson
Twitter Handle	@Emerson_Knives
Instagram Handle	@EmersonKnivesInc
Facebook Handle	@EmersonKnives
LinkedIn Handle	company/ emerson-knives-incorporated
YouTube Channel	@EmersonKnives
Website	**emersonknives.com**
Industry	Knives, Apparel, Gear, Coffee
What Makes Them Conservative	Everything!!

19. 1ˢᵗ Phorm

1ˢᵗ Phorm is a $200 million company run by a family of patriots, the Frisellas of St. Louis. CEO Andy Frisella is the host of the top-rated Real AF podcast, where he speaks out against the lockdowns and the insane masking and vaccine policies of the various levels of government.

Andy and his team are champions for freedom, America, and success. He kicks ass and he is always standing up for America. He and his company deserve your support!!! Their products are awesome, and they imbue everything they do with an optimistic, can-do spirit.

Company Name	1ˢᵗ Phorm
CEO	Andy Frisella
Twitter Handle	@1stPhorm
Instagram Handle	@1stPhorm
Facebook Handle	@1stPhorm
LinkedIn Handle	/company/1ˢᵗ-phorm-international
YouTube Channel	1ˢᵗ Phorm
Website	**1stPhorm.com**
Industry	Supplements, Health & Wellness Products, Gear
What Makes Them Conservative	They explicitly support freedom, conservative values and causes in all they do

20. GiveSendGo

"In 2014, three siblings had an idea. What would it look like if we took the newly popular idea of crowdfunding and stretched it beyond just funding help for people's material needs and providing hope for people's spiritual needs? Out of those discussions, GiveSendGo was born."

"Year after year, we kept running the race in obedience and with persistence waiting for the day GiveSendGo.com would take off. Little did we know God was just preparing us for the plans he had for us. At the end of the summer of 2020 during the middle of a pandemic, we watched as GiveSendGo was thrust into the political spotlight for allowing a campaign that mainstream media had shut down and was censoring. Unbeknownst to us, we had stepped onto a battlefield and had to take a stand. After much prayer, discussion, and counsel a decision was made. GiveSendGo was created for such a time as this. Not to take one side or another politically, but in the middle of a divided political culture, we were to be focused on the very reason we started GiveSendGo, to share the Hope of Jesus through crowdfunding to everyone who comes to our platform. That continues to be our focus as we stand for freedom.'

GiveSendGo allowed the Truckers of the Freedom Convoy to raise money to fund their protests. They withstood pressure from the Canadian and the US governments to do so. NEVER use anyone but GiveSendGo for crowdfunding!

Company Name	GiveSendGo
CEO	Jacob Wells & Heather Wilson
Twitter Handle	@GiveSendGo
Instagram Handle	@GiveSendGo
Facebook Handle	@GiveSendGo
LinkedIn Handle	/company/GiveSendGo-com
YouTube Channel	GiveSendGo
Website	**GiveSendGo.com**
Industry	Crowd Funding
What Makes Them Conservative	Pro Freedom & Free Speech. Allows conservatives to crowdfund. Funded the Freedom Convoy

Enemies of Wokism

These companies are all pro-American, and anti-woke. They keep politics out of the boardroom and out of the way they run their companies. They donate to Republicans and conservatives, and they deliver top-notch products and services to their customers. When you spend money with them, you better believe that it will NOT be going to causes you don't support, and it WILL be going to people and causes that align with your values. Many of these companies are also publicly traded, and you can invest in their securities versus the securities of the woke companies that don't share your values.

As always, check with your investment advisors when making investment decisions. We are not investment advisors, and nothing we say here should be construed as professional investment advice.

21. Kohler Co.

Kohler Co., founded in 1873 by John Michael Kohler, is a prominent American manufacturing company based in Kohler, Wisconsin, with over 40,000 employees worldwide. Kohler is best known for its plumbing products, but the company also manufactures furniture, cabinetry, tile, engines, and generators. Destination Kohler also owns various hospitality establishments in the United States and Scotland. In 2018, Kohler became a sponsor of the storied English soccer club Manchester United. As the club's sleeve sponsor, they prominently displayed the Kohler logo on all Manchester United jerseys. Kohler, a privately held corporation, does not adhere to the far-left ESG nonsense the left has forced many publicly traded corporations to adopt. Instead, they donate to conservative causes and politicians exclusively.

Company Name	Kohler Co.
CEO	K. David Kohler
Twitter Handle	@Kohler
Instagram Handle	@kohler
Facebook Handle	@KohlerCo
LinkedIn Handle	/company/kohler/
YouTube Channel	KOHLER
Website	**kohlercompany.com**
Industry	Plumbing Fixtures
What Makes Them Conservative	100% of its contributions go to Republicans and Conservatives

22. Cintas

Cintas is an American corporation headquartered in Cincinnati, Ohio, which provides a range of products and services to businesses, including uniforms, mats, mops, cleaning and restroom supplies, first aid and safety products, fire extinguishers and testing, and safety courses. Cintas is a publicly held company traded on the Nasdaq Global Select Market under the symbol CTAS and is a component of the Standard & Poor's 500 Index. The company is one of the largest in the industry, with over 40,000 employees in 2020. In 2020, the company reported $7.09 billion in total revenue, and they are #410 on the Fortune 500.

As a publicly held company, they adhere to Diversity and Inclusion and ESG standards. A closer look at how they do it shows that they mean to help clean up the environment and hire and include minorities, women, and veterans. They have been doing it since before it was trendy. The Framer family, who founded Cintas and still owns a big chunk of the company, is deeply conservative and donates large amounts to conservative causes and candidates. If you need their services, you should do business with Cintas and consider investing in their stock. As always, speak to your professional investment advisor before making any investment decisions, and do your own research and due diligence!

Company Name	Cintas Corporation
CEO	Todd M. Schneider
Twitter Handle	@CintasCorp
Instagram Handle	@cintas_corp
Facebook Handle	@Cintas
LinkedIn Handle	/company/cintas/
YouTube Channel	Cintas
Website	**cintas.com**
Stock Symbol	**CTAS (NASDAQ)**
Industry	Business Services
What Makes Them Conservative	Donates a large amount to Conservative causes

23. Duke Cannon Supply

We love these guys! They are everything an American company should be. We are just going to reproduce what they say about themselves from their website and urge you to buy their grooming products every day, and all day long, for yourself or for the men you love in your life. They make grooming products for men.

"IN A WORLD OF WEAK HANDSHAKES, HERE'S A FINGER-CRUSHING INTRODUCTION.

Duke Cannon hails from a simpler time. A time when the term handyman was redundant. A time when chivalry and patriotism weren't considered old-fashioned. A time when you never put the word salad next to bar.

But something happened along the way. Men were encouraged to put down their lug wrenches and pick up their phones to hashtag for help. Substance was replaced by the flash of guys taking selfies. And instead of getting up before dawn to build railroads, men started going to the gym at 9 a.m. to ride pretend bicycles. As any historian worth his salt will tell you, this country was built by folks with a sense of purpose. Duke Cannon's purpose is simple: to make superior-quality grooming goods that meet the high standards of hard-working men. Our products are tested by soldiers, not boy bands. And they're made in a little place we like to call the United States of America.

We value things like hard work, family, community, bacon and country; we champion builders, creators, sledge hammerers, holders of doors and fixers of toilets; we have the utmost respect for teachers and farmers and soldiers and first responders—so it's no wonder good folks feel right at home in Duke Cannon Country."

Company Name	Duke Cannon Supply Co.
CEO	Ryan O'Connell
Twitter Handle	@DukeCannon
Instagram Handle	@dukecannon
Facebook Handle	@DukeCannonSupplyCo
LinkedIn Handle	/company/dukecannon/
YouTube Channel	Duke Cannon Supply Co.
Website	**dukecannon.com**
Industry	Retail
What Makes Them Conservative	Supports Military Organizations with donations and products

24. Gab

Gab is a free speech alternative to Twitter. It has been falsely smeared by far-left forces as "racist" and "anti-Semitic", despite many prominent Jewish conservatives and supporters of the state of Israel (including both of us) using Gab as a platform. Gab, unlike the old Twitter regime and Facebook, does not censor people for having opinions it disagrees with.

We neither agree nor disagree with the opinions of Gab. But we applaud them for standing up for free expression and encourage you to use their platform.

Company Name	Gab
CEO	Andrew Torba
Twitter Handle	@getongab
Instagram Handle	@gabgeneral
Facebook Handle	N/A
LinkedIn Handle	/company/gab-ai-inc./
YouTube Channel	N/A
Website	**gab.com**
Industry	Social Networking
What Makes Them Conservative	Stands up for the quintessential American value of freedom of speech.

25. Epik

Rob Monster founded Epik in 2009 as the company's chief executive officer. The company is in Sammamish, Washington. As of May 2021, Epik is the 21st largest domain registrar in the United States and the 48th largest globally, as measured by the number of domains registered through the company.

Epik has been falsely smeared by far-left sites like Wikipedia and others as "far-right" and "anti-Semitic". Their favorite tactic against companies and individuals that stand up for American values like free speech, such as Epik, is to smear them and try to shut them up.

Keep using Epik!

Company Name	Epik
CEO	Rob Monster
Twitter Handle	@EpikDotCom
Instagram Handle	@EpikDotCom
Facebook Handle	@EpikDotCom
LinkedIn Handle	/company/epik.com/
YouTube Channel	epik
Website	**epik.com**
Industry	Domain Registrar and Web Hosting
What Makes Them Conservative	Hosts Gab citing free speech rights

26. J. Fletcher Creamer & Son, Inc.

J. Fletcher Creamer & Son, Inc. was founded in Fort Lee, New Jersey in 1923. The company evolved from a small Ford truck running deliveries and performing miscellaneous tasks to one of the country's leading contractors, working with many business, government, and non-profit organizations. They are a division of the API Group, a publicly traded company on the Nasdaq.

The company is a non-woke organization that deserves your support!

Company Name	J.Fletcher Creamer & Son Inc.
CEO	Joseph Walsh
Twitter Handle	@JF_Creamer
Instagram Handle	@j.fletchercreamer
Facebook Handle	@jfcson
LinkedIn Handle	/company/j.-fletcher-creamer-&-son/
YouTube Channel	N/A
Website	**jfcson.com**
Stock Symbol	APG (NASDAQ)
Industry	Full-Service Contracting Company
What Makes Them Conservative	97% of its' donations go to Conservatives

27. Outback Steakhouse

Outback Steakhouse is an Australian-themed American casual dining restaurant chain, serving American cuisine, based in Tampa, Florida. The chain has over 1,600 locations in 23 countries throughout North and South America, Asia, and Australia. It was founded in March 1988 with its first location in Tampa by Bob Basham, Chris T. Sullivan, Trudy Cooper, and Tim Gannon. It was owned and operated in the United States by OSI Restaurant Partners until it was acquired by Bloomin' Brands, and by other franchise and venture agreements internationally. Their annual revenues are $3.9 billion. Bloomin' Brands is a publicly traded stock on the Nasdaq under the symbol BLMN.

The company and its founders are major contributors, via the Outback Steakhouse PAC, to the Republican Party, contributing $303,015 and $334,197 for the 2000 and 2004 election cycles, respectively. The Outback Steakhouse PAC itself is one of the largest donors in the food and beverage sector, second only to the National Restaurant Association, which itself represents 300,000 restaurants. They deserve your support! Go eat there!!

Company Name	Outback Steakhouse
CEO	David J. Deno
Twitter Handle	@Outback
Instagram Handle	@outback
Facebook Handle	@outback
LinkedIn Handle	/company/outback-steakhouse/
YouTube Channel	Outback Steakhouse
Website	**outback.com**
Stock Symbol	**BLMN (NASDAQ)**
Industry	Restaurant Chain
What Makes Them Conservative	Supports and contributes to conservative causes

28. Sheetz, Inc.

Sheetz, Inc. is an American chain of convenience stores and coffee shops owned by the Sheetz family, with over 660 locations. The stores sell custom food, beverages and convenience store items, with all locations having offered 24/7 service since the 1980s. Nearly all of them sell gasoline; a few locations are full-scale truck stops, including showers and a laundromat. Sheetz's headquarters are in Altoona, Pennsylvania, with stores located in Pennsylvania, West Virginia, Maryland, Ohio, Virginia, and North Carolina.

Sheetz deserves your patronage!

Company Name	Sheetz
CEO	Stanton R. Sheetz
Twitter Handle	@sheetz
Instagram Handle	@sheetz
Facebook Handle	@sheetz
LinkedIn Handle	/company/sheetz/
YouTube Channel	Sheetz
Website	sheetz.com
Industry	Convenience Store
What Makes Them Conservative	Owned by a Republican family, donated hundreds of thousands of dollars to the GOP in 2020.

29. Menards

Menards is a home improvement retail company headquartered in Eau Claire, Wisconsin. Menards is owned by founder John Menard, Jr. through his privately held company, Menard, Inc. They have revenues of $11.8 billion, and over 45,000 employees.

The company has 335 stores in 15 states: Illinois, Indiana, Iowa, Kansas, Kentucky, Michigan, Minnesota, Missouri, Nebraska, North Dakota, Ohio, South Dakota, West Virginia, Wisconsin, and Wyoming.

In 2016, Menard, Inc. was ranked 37th on Forbes' list of "America's Largest Private Companies". That same year, Menard was ranked 45th on the National Retail Federation's list of "100 Top Retailers". In 2018, Menards was ranked by J.D. Power as "highest in customer satisfaction among home improvement retail stores".

The founder is a staunch conservative and the company has supported conservative causes throughout its existence. They deserve your support!

Company Name	Menards
CEO	John Menard, Jr.
Twitter Handle	@Menards
Instagram Handle	@menardshomeimprovement
Facebook Handle	@MenardsHomeImprovement
LinkedIn Handle	/company/menards/
YouTube Channel	Menards
Website	**menards.com**
Industry	Home Improvement Company
What Makes Them Conservative	Conservative views and supports conservative causes

30. OAN

One America News Network "OAN" delivers a credible source for national and international news 24/7, including breaking political, business and entertainment headlines. One America News Network is owned by Herring Networks, Inc. Herring Networks, Inc. is a family-owned and operated, independent media company focused on providing high quality national television programming to consumers via its national cable networks. The for-profit company was established in 2004 and has its primary production operations in California and Washington, DC.

Direct TV, under pressure from the Far Left, cancelled its contract carrying OAN. They are a great company, deliver news from a conservative point of view, and are worthy of your support.

Company Name	One America News Network
CEO	Robert Herring Sr.
Twitter Handle	@OANN
Instagram Handle	@one_america_news
Facebook Handle	@OneAmericaNewsNetwork
LinkedIn Handle	/company/ one-america-news-network/
YouTube Channel	One America News Network
Website	**oann.com**
Industry	Media
What Makes Them Conservative	Praised by Donald Trump, airs stories conservative viewers want to watch, but cannot find on other cable channels

Real American Companies

T hese next group of companies are all defenders of traditional American values. They have publicly taken a stance in favor of freedom, free expression, and free enterprise. They have taken the slings and arrows from the evil left and are still standing up for America and all that she stands for.

God bless them all, and please use their services when you need the types of products and services they have to offer.

31. Russell Stover Chocolates

Russell Stover Chocolates, Inc., founded by Russell Stover, an American chemist and entrepreneur, and his wife Clara Stover in 1923, is an American supplier of candy, chocolate, and confections. The corporate headquarters are in Kansas City, Missouri.

In July 2014 the company was acquired by the Swiss chocolatier Lindt & Sprüngli for $1.6 billion. The company operates as an independent subsidiary and is still based in Kansas City.

Their website states "We proudly manufacture our chocolates in the heartland of the United States of America and have maintained this tradition since Clara Stover founded the company in 1923. We even make most of our boxes here, too. Our factories located in Kansas, Missouri, Texas, and Colorado employ generations of candy makers and box builders who take pride in making chocolates for our neighbors near and far."

"We source some of our ingredients at home in the United States, while others are sourced globally. Our cream and milk come from Oklahoma, cherries from Michigan and Oregon, and peanuts from across the South, for example."

"We are honored that our chocolates have been part of American traditions and culture for decades, and proud to manufacture them at home in America."

This is a company that deserves your support!

Company Name	Russell Stover Chocolates
CEO	Andreas Pfluger
Twitter Handle	@hirussellstover
Instagram Handle	@russellstoverus
Facebook Handle	@russellstoverus
LinkedIn Handle	/company/russell-stover-chocolates/
YouTube Channel	Russell Stover
Website	**russellstover.com**
Stock Symbol	**LISN (SWX)**
Industry	Food
What Makes Them Conservative	Conservative views and supports conservative causes

32. Uline

Uline is a privately held American company which offers shipping and other business supplies. Uline was founded in 1980 by Richard and Elizabeth Uihlein. It has more than 8,000 employees and is headquartered in Pleasant Prairie, Wisconsin. The company has distribution centers throughout the United States, Canada, and Mexico. Its annual revenues are approaching $8.8 billion a year.

Liz and Richard Uihlein are patriots and mega-donors to conservative and Republican causes. The company and its employees have also extensively donated to conservative and Republican-affiliated political action committees; they were among the largest contributors to political campaigns during the 2020 election cycle, contributing over $31 million before June 2020. They massively deserve your support!

Company Name	Uline
CEO	Richard E. Uihlein
Twitter Handle	@uline
Instagram Handle	@uline_shippingsupplies
Facebook Handle	@Uline
LinkedIn Handle	/company/uline/
YouTube Channel	Uline
Website	**uline.com**
Industry	Supplies
What Makes Them Conservative	Supports Conservative causes, some of their trucks have the bible reference "John 3:16"

33. Brave

Brave is a free and open-source web browser developed by Brave Software, Inc. based on the Chromium web browser. Brave is a privacy-focused browser, which automatically blocks online advertisements and website trackers in its default settings. It also provides users the choice to turn on optional ads that pay users for their attention in the form of Basic Attention Tokens (BAT) cryptocurrency. Users can then send contributions to websites and content creators, which support BAT in the form of tips along with the ability to keep the cryptocurrency they earned.

Brave Software's headquarters are in San Francisco, California.

As of July 2022, Brave has more than 62 million monthly active users, 19.2 million daily active users and a network of more than 1.4 million content creators.

Brendan Eich, the CEO, is a veteran of the cancel culture wars, having been kicked out of a previous company he founded for donating to causes supporting traditional marriage.

Company Name	Brave
CEO	Brendan Eich
Twitter Handle	@brave
Instagram Handle	@bebravebrowser
Facebook Handle	@BraveSoftware
LinkedIn Handle	/company/brave-software/
YouTube Channel	Brave
Website	**brave.com**
Industry	Internet
What Makes Them Conservative	Blocks data-grabbing ads and trackers. Avoids content censorship

34. Omni Hotels & Resorts

Omni Hotels & Resorts is a privately-held international luxury hotel company based in Dallas, Texas. The company was founded in 1958 as Dunfey Hotels and operates 50 properties in the United States, Canada, and Mexico, totalling over 20,010 rooms and employing more than 23,000 people. Their leadership is deeply conservative and donates exclusively to Republican and conservative causes.

Go stay at their hotels!!

Company Name	Omni Hotels & Resorts
CEO	Robert Rowling
Twitter Handle	@OmniHotels
Instagram Handle	@omnihotels
Facebook Handle	@omnihotels
LinkedIn Handle	/company/omni-hotels/
YouTube Channel	Omni Hotels and Resorts
Website	**omnihotels.com**
Industry	Hotel
What Makes Them Conservative	Organization donation went 100% Republican in 2020

35. **ABC Supply Co.**

ABC Supply Co., Inc. is a major, private American roofing supply company based in Beloit, Wisconsin. It also sells windows, gutters, and siding for residential and commercial buildings and is the largest roofing and vinyl siding wholesale distributor in the United States.

The company was founded in 1982 by Ken and Diane Hendricks. It grew from a single store in Wisconsin to having over 700 branches in 49 states nationwide, and sales of over $11 billion.

The company has won the Gallup Great Workplace Award for the eleven consecutive years, from 2007 to 2017.

Diane Hendricks is a megadonor to conservative and Republican causes. She was among the 10 largest individual contributors to Donald Trump during the 2020 elections.

Buy your roofing supplies here!

Company Name	ABC Supply
CEO	Keith Rozolis
Twitter Handle	N/A
Instagram Handle	N/A
Facebook Handle	@ABCSupply
LinkedIn Handle	/company/abc-supply/
YouTube Channel	ABC Supply Inc. Co.
Website	**abcsupply.com**
Industry	Supply Company
What Makes Them Conservative	CEO raised money for Trump presidential campaign

36. Ace Hardware

Ace Hardware Corporation is an American hardware retailers' cooperative based in Oak Brook, Illinois. It is the world's largest hardware retail cooperative and non-grocery American retail cooperative.

In 1924, entrepreneurs Richard Hesse, E. Gunnard Lindquist, Frank Burke and Oscar Fisher united their Chicago, Illinois, hardware stores into "Ace Stores" to increase buying power and profits. They named the company after the ace fighter pilots of World War I, men who had shot down at least 5 enemy planes in aerial combat, and had the confidence to overcome all odds.

The company changed its name to "Ace Hardware Corporation" in 1931. It grew dramatically following World War II, more than tripling its sales between the late 1940s and 1959. After the retirement of longtime president and cofounder Richard Hesse in 1973, Ace was sold to its retailers, becoming a retailer-owned cooperative. It first reached $1 billion in wholesale sales in 1985 and $5 billion in 2015.

Ace Hardware is an American company and is worthy of your support! Buy from them!

Company Name	Ace Hardware
CEO	John Venhuizen
Twitter Handle	@AceHardwardeCO
Instagram Handle	@acehardwardeco
Facebook Handle	@acehardwardeco
LinkedIn Handle	/company/acehardwarecorp/
YouTube Channel	Ace Hardware
Website	**acehardware.com**
Industry	Hardware Store Company
What Makes Them Conservative	Supports Conservative causes

37. LendingTree

LendingTree is an online lending marketplace headquartered in Charlotte, NC. The business platform allows potential borrowers to connect with multiple loan operators to find optimal terms for loans, credit cards, deposit accounts, insurance, etc. LendingTree allows borrowers to shop and compare competitive rates and terms across an array of financial products. Founded in 1996 by Doug Lebda, who remains the CEO to this day, the company has offices in the San Francisco Bay Area, New York City, Chicago, Seattle and many other cities. LendingTree is a publicly traded company on the Nasdaq, with the ticker symbol TREE.

They have refrained from embracing the woke, ESG agenda of anti-freedom organizations like Black Rock. They deserve your support!

Company Name	Lending Tree
CEO	Doug Lebda
Twitter Handle	@LendingTree
Instagram Handle	@lendingtree
Facebook Handle	@LendingTree
LinkedIn Handle	/company/lendingtree/
YouTube Channel	LendingTree
Website	**LendingTree.com**
Stock Symbol	**TREE (NASDAQ)**
Industry	Lending Marketplace
What Makes Them Conservative	CEO raised money for a pro-Trump super PAC

38. Advance Auto Parts

Advance Auto Parts, Inc. is an American automotive aftermarket parts provider. Headquartered in Raleigh, North Carolina, it serves both professional installers and do-it-yourself (DIY) customers. Advance operates 4,912 stores and 150 Worldpac branches in the United States and Canada. The Company also serves 1,250 independently owned Carquest branded stores across Canada and the United States, as well as Mexico, the Bahamas, Turks, Caicos and the British Virgin Islands. They are a publicly traded company on the NYSE, with the ticker symbol AAP.

The company retails various brand names, original equipment manufacturer (OEM) and private label automotive replacement parts, accessories, batteries and maintenance items for domestic and imported cars, vans, sport utility vehicles and light and heavy-duty trucks.

They are a Fortune 500 company and mercifully have the courage to live by traditional American values of freedom, free expression, and capitalism. They deserve your support!

Company Name	Advance Auto Parts
CEO	Thomas R. Greco
Twitter Handle	@AdvanceAuto
Instagram Handle	@advanceautoparts
Facebook Handle	@advanceautoparts
LinkedIn Handle	/company/advance-auto-parts/
YouTube Channel	Advance Auto Parts
Website	**advanceautoparts.com**
Stock Symbol	**AAP (NYSE)**
Industry	Automotive Company
What Makes Them Conservative	Supports conservative causes

39. Amway

Amway (short for "American Way") is an American multi-level marketing (MLM) company that sells health, beauty, and home care products. The company was founded in 1959 by Jay Van Andel and Richard DeVos and is based in Ada, Michigan. Amway and its sister companies under Alticor reported sales of $8.4 billion in 2019. It conducts business through several affiliated companies in more than a hundred countries and territories.

Betsy DeVos, the wife of founder Richard DeVos, served in the Trump Administration as the Secretary of Education. Amway and its founders are conservative to the core, and champion freedom and free enterprise.

They deserve your support!

Company Name	Amway
CEO	Milind Pant
Twitter Handle	@Amway
Instagram Handle	@amwayus
Facebook Handle	@amway
LinkedIn Handle	/company/amway/
YouTube Channel	Amway US
Website	**amwayglobal.com**
Industry	Multi-level Marketing
What Makes Them Conservative	100% of its contributions go to Republicans and Conservatives. Leftists boycott this company

40. BF Goodrich

BF Goodrich is an American tire company. Originally part of the industrial conglomerate Goodrich Corporation, it was acquired in 1990 (along with Uniroyal, then The Uniroyal Goodrich Tire Company) by the French tire maker Michelin. Before the sale, BF Goodrich was the first American tire manufacturer to make radial tires. It made tires for the then-new Winton car from Winton Motor Carriage Company.

BF Goodrich tires have been fitted to several noteworthy historical vehicles:

- In 1903 the first car to cross the United States was fitted with BF Goodrich tires.
- In 1927 Charles Lindbergh's airplane, the "Spirit of St. Louis," which made the first successful solo non-stop flight across the Atlantic, was fitted with BF Goodrich tires. In 1977 the space shuttle Columbia was fitted with BF Goodrich tires during construction.
- BF Goodrich has been involved in several competitions and enjoyed success with 28 overall victories at the Baja California Competitions and 13 times winner of the Paris–Dakar Rally.

They are a big American corporation resisting the ESG scourge and sticking to business. They are worthy of your support!

Company Name	**B.F. Goodrich**
CEO	Marshall Larsen
Twitter Handle	@BFGoodrichTires
Instagram Handle	@bfgoodrichtires
Facebook Handle	@BFGoodrichTires
LinkedIn Handle	/company/bf-goodrich/about/
YouTube Channel	BFGoodrich
Website	**bfgoodrichtires.com**
Stock Symbol	**ML (EURONEXT PARIS)**
Industry	Tires
What Makes Them Conservative	97% of its contributions go to Republicans and Conservatives

41. Founder Sport Group

The Founder Sport Group brings together Badger Sport, Alleson Athletic, Garb Athletics and Teamwork Athletic along with nearly 150 years of collective experience to better outfit teams, players, family and fans.

They are patriotic, pro-American, and anti-human trafficking. They have showed real guts in cutting ties with Communist China. Buy their gear!

Company Name	Founder Sport Group
CEO	John Anton
Twitter Handle	@badger_sport
Instagram Handle	@badgersportofficial
Facebook Handle	@badgersportswear
LinkedIn Handle	/company/badger-sport/
YouTube Channel	Badger Sportswear
Website	**foundersport.com**
Industry	Fashion
What Makes Them Conservative	Cut ties in Red China after discovering a company that was affiliated with them uses concentration camps for targeted members of ethnic minorities persecuted by the government

42. Black Rifle Coffee Company

Black Rifle Coffee Company (BRCC) is a coffee company based in Salt Lake City, Utah, owned by former members of the armed forces of the United States. It gained national attention in 2017, when it employed about 50 people, after pledging to hire 10,000 veterans in response to Starbucks's pledge to hire 10,000 refugees.

Black Rifle Coffee Company's corporate image is built on its conservative politics and supporting veterans. Over half of its staff are former military. It is a publicly traded company on the NYSE, and the Stock Ticker Symbol is BRCC.

The company maintains a pro-military, pro-gun, pro-police image and has publicly supported the politics of former US President Donald Trump through actions such as publishing a (since-deleted) blog post that supported Trump's then-current proposal of an immigration ban from Muslim-majority countries. The company's political stance has attracted attention from Fox News, and it has been endorsed by conservative broadcast personalities Sean Hannity and Donald Trump Jr.

BRCC did garner some blowback when it distanced itself from Kyle Rittenhouse for wearing one of its t-shirts during his trial for murder. Rittenhouse was acquitted of all charges because all he did was act in self-defense against a bunch of thugs and pedophiles who tried to kill him. This was not BRCC's finest moment, but it has since backtracked on how it handled the Rittenhouse situation.

Company Name	Black Rifle Coffee
CEO	Evan Hafer
Twitter Handle	@blackriflecoffee
Instagram Handle	@blackriflecoffee
Facebook Handle	N/A
LinkedIn Handle	/company/ black-rifle-coffee-company/
YouTube Channel	Black Rifle Coffee Company
Website	**blackriflecoffee.com**
Stock Symbol	**BRCC (NYSE)**
Industry	Coffee Company
What Makes Them Conservative	Conservative company; supports Conservative causes

43. Blue Bell Creameries

A group of local businessmen in Brenham, Texas, decided to establish the Brenham Creamery Company and make butter from excess cream brought in by area farmers in 1907. A few years later, the creamery began making ice cream and delivering it to neighbors by horse and wagon. It was in 1930 that the company changed its name to Blue Bell Creameries after the native Texas bluebell wildflower. Butter was produced until 1958 when Blue Bell began to focus full time on making ice cream.

Blue Bell employs over 1000 people and generates $700 Million in annual revenue. They are a conservative company, with no wokeism whatsoever in their corporate DNA. They deserve your support! Go have some Blue Bell ice cream on a hot day!

Company Name	Blue Bell Creameries
CEO	Ricky Dickson
Twitter Handle	@ILoveBlueBell
Instagram Handle	@bluebellicecream
Facebook Handle	@bluebellcreamery
LinkedIn Handle	/company/blue-bell-creameries/
YouTube Channel	N/A
Website	**bluebell.com**
Industry	Creamery
What Makes Them Conservative	Conservative company; supports conservative causes

44. Bob Evans Farms

Bob Evans founded Bob Evans Restaurants in 1948 when he began processing and packaging sausage for his small diner in Gallipolis, Ohio. Early operations were based at his farm in the Rio Grande. As the reputation of his sausage grew, so did the number of guests who visited his farm to buy it in bulk. As a result, friends and family partnered together to establish Bob Evans Farms, Inc., in 1953. The increased traffic led him to build the first company restaurant at the farm in 1962 which was named "The Sausage Shop".

Today, the company has over 440 restaurants across the USA. They don't kowtow to the woke mob, and support conservatives and conservative causes. They deserve your support!

Company Name	Bob Evans Farms
CEO	Saed Mohseni
Twitter Handle	@BobEvansFarms
Instagram Handle	@bobevansfarms
Facebook Handle	@bobevans
LinkedIn Handle	/company/bob-evans/
YouTube Channel	Bob Evans Farms
Website	**bobevans.com**
Industry	Restaurants
What Makes Them Conservative	Conservative company; supports conservative causes

45. Breitbart News

Founded by the late, great Andrew Breitbart, Breitbart is a conservative news juggernaut. They fearlessly cover the stories that the lame-stream media won't, and they are responsible for helping normal Americans get the truth, perhaps more than any other media outlet in the country.

We both read Breitbart regularly, and we highly recommend that you support them, too!

Company Name	Breitbart News
CEO	Larry Solov
Twitter Handle	@BreitbartNews
Instagram Handle	@wearebreitbart
Facebook Handle	@Breitbart
LinkedIn Handle	N/A
YouTube Channel	Breitbart News
Website	**breitbart.com**
Industry	Media
What Makes Them Conservative	Conservative News Outlet, founded by a legendary conservative warrior

The Patriotic Core

T his next group of companies have all been founded by men and women who believe in the promise of America and the free enterprise system under which she operates. Every single one of these firms is an enemy of the woke and a friend of the patriot. Every single one of these firms has products and services that you probably need and can use. Every single one of these firms deserves your dollars more than the woke corporations that hate you and all that you stand for.

Support them!

46. Forbes

Forbes is a legendary American business magazine owned by Integrated Whale Media Investments and the iconic Forbes family. Published eight times a year, it features articles on finance, industry, investing, and marketing topics. Forbes also reports on related subjects such as technology, communications, science, politics, and law. It is based in Jersey City, New Jersey. Competitors in the national business magazine category include the woke Fortune and Bloomberg Businessweek.

Forbes is best known for its lists and rankings, including the richest Americans (*the Forbes 400*), *America's Wealthiest Celebrities*, the world's top companies (*the Forbes Global 2000*), Forbes list of the *World's Most Powerful People*, and *The World's Billionaires*. Its motto is "Change the World". The chair and editor-in-chief of Forbes is Steve Forbes, former Republican candidate for President. They have been a conservative and pro-American magazine for nearly 100 years. Check them out and support them!

Company Name	Forbes Magazine
CEO	Mike Federle
Twitter Handle	@Forbes
Instagram Handle	@Forbes
Facebook Handle	@Forbes
LinkedIn Handle	/company/forbes-magazine/
YouTube Channel	Forbes
Website	**forbes.com**
Industry	Magazine
What Makes Them Conservative	Conservative company; supports conservative causes

47. Regnery Publishing

Regnery Publishing is the country's leading publisher of conservative books. Since Henry Regnery founded the company back in 1947, they have focused on publishing books that challenge the status quo, books that spark a debate and books that get people talking about the issues and questions we face as a country. They are now a division of the Salem Media Group.

Regnery has been a major force within the conservative movement, publishing such authors as Russell Kirk (*The Conservative Mind*), William F. Buckley, Jr. (*God and Man at Yale*), Whittaker Chambers (*Witness*), and many other giants of American conservatism. Regnery has also led the modern resurgence of conservative publishing over the past couple of decades. Their list of authors reads like a "who's who" of conservative thought and action; including Wayne Allyn Root, Ann Coulter, David Limbaugh, Michelle Malkin, Dinesh D'Souza, Newt Gingrich, Mark Steyn, Mark Levin, Ed Klein, David Horowitz, Laura Ingraham, Donald Trump, and many more. Regnery has boasted one of the best batting averages in the publishing business – placing more than fifty books on the New York Times bestseller list, including numerous books at #1.

Company Name	Regnery Publishing
CEO	Thomas Spence
Twitter Handle	@Regnery
Instagram Handle	@regnerypub
Facebook Handle	@RegneryBooks
LinkedIn Handle	/company/regnery-publishing/
YouTube Channel	Regnery Publishing
Website	**regnery.com**
Industry	Publishing Company
What Makes Them Conservative	Only supports conservative authors and conservative companies.

48. Kahr Arms

Kahr Arms is an American small arms manufacturer specializing in compact and mid-size semi-automatic pistols chambered for popular cartridges, including .380 ACP, 9mm Luger, .40 S&W and .45 ACP. Kahr pistols feature polymer or stainless-steel frames, single-stack magazines and double-action-only striker firing actions. Kahr Arms is part of the Kahr Firearms Group, a US-based firearms manufacturer, which also includes Thompson Auto-Ordnance and Magnum Research, the maker of the iconic Desert Eagle handgun. The Kahr Firearms Group company headquarters is in Greeley, Pennsylvania, with a manufacturing facility in Worcester, Massachusetts.

Kahr Arms was founded by Justin Moon, who is CEO and president. He is the son of Sun Myung Moon, founder of the Unification Church and brother to Hyung Jin Moon, pastor of the World Peace and Unification Sanctuary Church. This is a family that has faced the evils of communism and understand the importance of a strong Bill of Rights. Every red-blooded American should own a gun and learn to safely and responsibly use one. Kahr Arms is a great company with excellent products!

Company Name	Kahr Arms
CEO	Justin Moon
Twitter Handle	@KahrFirearms
Instagram Handle	@kahrfirearms
Facebook Handle	@KahrArms
LinkedIn Handle	/company/ kahr-arms-auto-ordnance/
YouTube Channel	Kahr Firearms Group
Website	**kahr.com**
Industry	Gun maker
What Makes Them Conservative	Hosts an annual free 2nd Amendment Festival. Family that owns the company knows first-hand the evils of liberalism.

49. Conservative Grounds

Conservative Grounds was launched after a barista at Starbucks asked 6 Police Officers to leave their coffee shop. Appalled by such actions, and spurred by the belief that this type of hatred towards law enforcement should NEVER happen again, Cliff Gephart and John Tatum gave birth to "the Grounds". The Founders had a desire to create a place where Conservatives would feel welcome and America would be loved. American Patriots deserve a place to congregate, converse and enjoy a beverage along with a pastry, snack, or sweet treat without having to choke it down with a dose of liberalism. Donald Trump, Jr. is a huge fan!

Conservative Grounds is a place to promote Conservative Values and an alternative to the Liberal Coffee shops that were the only option until NOW. They welcome all those who no longer wish to support coffee houses that funnel their monies to liberal policies and politicians. DO NOT inadvertently give your money to causes you are against, stop supporting Liberal Companies that don't have the same values as you.

Company Name	Conservative Grounds
CEO	Cliff Gephart (Co-CEO) John Tatum (Co-CEO)
Twitter Handle	@therightcoffee
Instagram Handle	@conservative_grounds
Facebook Handle	@conservativegrounds
LinkedIn Handle	N/A
YouTube Channel	N/A
Website	conservativegrounds.com
Industry	Coffee shops
What Makes Them Conservative	Chain of conservative coffee shops supporting conservative causes

50. Curves

Curves was founded by Gary Heavin and his wife, Diane. They opened their first Curves in Harlingen, Texas, in 1992. This new concept of 30-minute fitness, strength training, weight-loss guidance, and an environment designed for women was immediately successful. By October 2006, Curves was said to have had over 10,000 locations worldwide, with 7,848 of those locations in the United States.

Curves fitness and weight loss facilities are designed specifically for and focused on women. The program is designed around circuit training, which utilizes hydraulic resistance equipment to achieve results. The strength training regimen is combined with cardiovascular training for a full body workout, with each class led by a 'Curves Coach'.

Curves also provide additional programs alongside their traditional gym workouts. For example, the Curves Nutrition and Weight Management Program is a fully integrated, personalized weight loss and weight management program with customizable meal plans and one-on-one coaching support alongside the Curves fitness program.

Curves founder Gary Heavin is unapologetically pro-life, having donated over $1 million to pro-life causes, and has financially supported other organizations that fight for the constitution and our rights. Curves is a company worthy of your support.

Company Name	Curves Fitness
CEO	Krishea Holloway
Twitter Handle	@Curves
Instagram Handle	@curvesofficial
Facebook Handle	@Curves
LinkedIn Handle	/company/curves/
YouTube Channel	Curves
Website	**curves.com**
Industry	Fitness Company
What Makes Them Conservative	Contributes to pro-life causes, boycotted by pro-abortion activists

51. Gold Gate Capital

Gold Gate Capital is a boutique family-owned company based in Los Angeles, California. They sell gold and silver to the public. Gold Gate Capital's company is based on conservative values, low taxes, de-regulation, free markets, and reducing government spending and debt. They also advertise on conservative media! Check them out! And buy your gold and silver from them!

Company Name	Gold Gate Capital
CEO	Kyle Winn
Twitter Handle	N/A
Instagram Handle	N/A
Facebook Handle	N/A
LinkedIn Handle	N/A
YouTube Channel	N/A
Website	GoldGateCapital.com
Industry	Gold & Silver Broker
What Makes Them Conservative	Free Market company, advertises on conservative shows

52. Ameo Life

Ameo Life is a wellness company that provides supplements and wellness products for health-conscious Americans. Their products are excellent. They advertise on conservative media, and they don't allow the woke left to bully them out of doing so. They are a great American company, and they deserve your support!

Ameo Life has a dedication to offering a unique approach to supplementation. Understanding what is making the body sick provides a better understanding of giving what the body needs to "heal naturally".

Ameo Life is dedicated to your health freedom and supplying natural supplementation that compliments the body's ability to heal naturally.

All products formulated by Ameo Life are free of chemicals, toxins and GMOs and supply the body with only the purest raw ingredients that support the immune and digestive systems.

Company Name	Ameo Life
CEO	Doug Godkin
Twitter Handle	(@AmeoLife)
Instagram Handle	(@AmeoLifeWellness)
Facebook Handle	(@LoveAmeoLife)
LinkedIn Handle	N/A
YouTube Channel	N/A
Website	**AmeoLife.com**
Industry	Wellness Company
What Makes Them Conservative	Contributes to pro-life causes, conservative causes, advertises on conservative shows

53. Mardel Christian & Education

Mardel Christian & Education is a privately owned chain of Christian bookstores, located mainly in the central and south-central United States.

The chain is owned by Mart Green, son of legendary Hobby Lobby founder David Green, and is based in Oklahoma City.

Along with LifeWay Christian Stores, it is one of the two largest chains of Christian bookstores (with LifeWay's decision to close its stores it will become the only major chain operating traditional retail outlets). These guys are the real deal! Shop with them! Their t-shirts rock!!

Company Name	Mardel Christian & Education
CEO	Mart Green
Twitter Handle	@Mardel_Inc
Instagram Handle	@Mardel_Inc
Facebook Handle	@Mardel
LinkedIn Handle	/company/mardel
YouTube Channel	@MardelTV
Website	**mardel.com**
Industry	Bookstores
What Makes Them Conservative	Contributes to pro-life causes, conservative causes, advertises on conservative shows

54. Dillard's

Dillard's, Inc. is an upscale American department store chain with approximately 282 stores in 29 states and headquartered in Little Rock, Arkansas. Currently, the largest number of stores are in the RED STATES of Texas with 57 and Florida with 42. The company also has stores in 27 more states; however, it is absent from the Northeast (Washington, D.C., and northward), most of the Upper Midwest (Michigan, Wisconsin, Minnesota), the Northwest, and most of California, aside from three stores in smaller cities. They are publicly traded on the NYSE.

These folks sell in the heartland! And they do not kowtow to the ESG crowd! They deserve your support!

Company Name	Dillard's
CEO	William T. Dillard II
Twitter Handle	@Dillards
Instagram Handle	@Dillards
Facebook Handle	@Dillards
LinkedIn Handle	/company/dillards/
YouTube Channel	Dillard's
Website	**dillards.com**
Stock Symbol	**DDS Class A (NYSE)**
Industry	Department Store
What Makes Them Conservative	Has sold Trump products, non-woke.

55. Domino's

Domino's was founded by legendary pro-life icon Tom Monaghan in 1960. He sold the company for $1 billion to Bain Capital in 1998. They are a publicly traded company on the NYSE, with the stock ticker symbol DPZ. But the company seems to be following Monaghan's pro-life steps. They are a huge pizza company, and they are resisting the calls of the woke.

If you like pizza, order from Domino's once in a while!

Company Name	Domino's Pizza
CEO	Richard E. Allison Jr.
Twitter Handle	@dominos
Instagram Handle	@dominos
Facebook Handle	@dominos
LinkedIn Handle	/company/dominos-pizza/
YouTube Channel	Domino's Pizza
Website	**dominos.com**
Stock Symbol	**DPZ (NYSE)**
Industry	Restaurant Chain
What Makes Them Conservative	Supports Conservatives and pro-life causes

56. Energized Health

Energized Health is a Health & Wellness Services company founded by John & Chelsea Jubilee. Since 1988, they have been dedicated to transforming the lives of thousands in their mission to get people healthy using inner cellular hydration. John struggled with his own weight for years while program after the program failed him. Completely frustrated, he invested years of research and developed a natural, simple, and scientific way to transform lives in 88 days using Inner Cellular Hydration. The co-author of this book, Wayne Allyn Root, used the program to lose 25 pounds of fat in only 88 days (and he also gained 10 pounds of muscle). He credits this program with changing his life.

They advertise on conservative media and deserve your support!

Company Name	Energized Health
CEO	John Jubilee
Twitter Handle	@JohnJubilee
Instagram Handle	@Energized.Health
Facebook Handle	@EnergizedHealth
LinkedIn Handle	N/A
YouTube Channel	N/A
Website	**EnergizedHealth.com**
Industry	Health & Wellness Services
What Makes Them Conservative	Supports Conservatives and pro-life causes, advertises on conservative media

57. Urban Outfitters

Urban Outfitters, Inc. (URBN) is a multinational lifestyle retail corporation headquartered in Philadelphia, Pennsylvania. It operates in the United States, Sweden, the United Kingdom, Spain, Denmark, France, Germany, Portugal, Ireland, Belgium, Canada, Italy, the Netherlands, Poland, and the United Arab Emirates.

The Urban Outfitters brand targets young adults with a merchandise mix of women's and men's fashion apparel, footwear, beauty and wellness products, accessories, activewear and gear, and housewares; as well as music (primarily vinyl records and cassettes).

The company was founded as the retail store **Free People** (great name!) by Richard Hayne, Judy Wicks and Scott Belair in 1970 as a project for an entrepreneurship class at the University of Pennsylvania. It was renamed Urban Outfitters and incorporated in 1976.

Urban Outfitters has all the right enemies, drawing criticism from far-left pressure groups like the NAACP and the Anti-Defamation League. They deserve your support!

Company Name	Urban Outfitters
CEO	Richard Hayne
Twitter Handle	@UrbanOutfitters
Instagram Handle	@urbanoutfitters
Facebook Handle	@urbanoutfitters
LinkedIn Handle	/company/urban-outfitters/
YouTube Channel	Urban Outfitters Television
Website	**urbanoutfitters.com**
Stock Symbol	**URBN (NASDAQ)**
Industry	Retail
What Makes Them Conservative	Financially supports conservative causes, refuses to support perverts!

58. Las Vegas Sands

Founded by legendary entrepreneur Sheldon Adelson, Las Vegas Sands Corporation is an American casino and resort company based in Paradise, Nevada. The resort features accommodations, gambling and entertainment, convention and exhibition facilities, restaurants, clubs, as well as an art and science museum in Singapore.

In addition, it has several resorts in Asia. Among the properties it developed in Asia, the Marina Bay Sands located in Singapore was added to the company's portfolio in 2010. Through its majority-owned subsidiary Sands China, the company owns several properties in Macao, including the Sands Macao, The Londoner Macao, The Venetian Macao, The Plaza Macao, and The Parisian Macao. It is the largest casino company worldwide.

Las Vegas Sands and their former Chairman (the late) Sheldon Adelson were the largest GOP donors over the past decade. Since 1992, Las Vegas Sands has contributed $70.5 million to federal campaigns, with 100% going to Republicans. They are publicly traded on the NYSE.

Go gamble at one of their properties!

Company Name	Las Vegas Sands Corp.
CEO	Robert Glen Goldstein
Twitter Handle	@LasVegasSands
Instagram Handle	@las_vegas_sands
Facebook Handle	@lasvegassands
LinkedIn Handle	/company/ las-vegas-sands-corporation/
YouTube Channel	Las Vegas Sands
Website	**sands.com**
Stock Symbol	**LVS (NYSE)**
Industry	Casinos and Resort
What Makes Them Conservative	Donated to many Conservative candidates and causes, supports Conservative principles

59. Dollar General

Dollar General Corporation is an American chain of variety stores headquartered in Goodlettsville, Tennessee. As of April 11, 2022, Dollar General operates 18,216 stores in the continental United States.

The Fortune 500 list welcomed Dollar General in 1999, and in 2020, it reached #112. Dollar General has grown to become one of the most profitable stores in the rural United States, with revenue reaching around $27 billion in 2019. They are not perfect from a conservative point of view, but they are mostly apolitical in their public pronouncements, and they do heavily donate to and support conservative causes. They are publicly traded on the NYSE. We are keeping our eye on them.

They deserve your support!

Company Name	Dollar General
CEO	Todd J. Vasos
Twitter Handle	@DollarGeneral
Instagram Handle	@dollargeneral
Facebook Handle	@dollargeneral
LinkedIn Handle	/company/dollar-general/
YouTube Channel	Dollar General
Website	**dollargeneral.com**
Stock Symbol	**DG (NYSE)**
Industry	Variety Store
What Makes Them Conservative	Conservative company; supports conservative causes

60. The Daily Wire

The Daily Wire is one of the fastest-growing digital media companies in America. They offer a full spectrum of programming, all the way from news and commentary to movie production and streaming of conservative-themed movies. Their content is amazing, and they deserve your support.

Stop watching CNN, CBS, ABC, and NBC and their online media content, and watch Daily Wire's instead. Cancel your Disney+ subscription.

Company Name	The Daily Wire
CEO	Ben Shapiro (Co-CEO) Jeremy Boering (Co-CEO)
Twitter Handle	@realDailyWire
Instagram Handle	@realdailywire
Facebook Handle	@DailyWire
LinkedIn Handle	/company/thedailywire/
YouTube Channel	The Daily Wire
Website	**dailywire.com**
Industry	Media & Entertainment
What Makes Them Conservative	Branched out into entertainment and is now producing movies that are conservative

Proud, Judeo-Christian & Conservative

There was a time when most American companies were proudly owned by men and women who embraced the nation's Judeo-Christian roots and reflected the values of this Judeo-Christian nation. Their owners were proud of their faith, and proudly reflected their faith in their businesses. These companies harken back to those days and offer products and services you use and need every day.

61. We The People Wine

We are just going to directly quote from their website:

"WE THE PEOPLE is an American brand dedicated to Conservative values. Our wine is made for Americans by Americans. American exceptionalism, free markets, free people, free speech and limited government are what we stand for.

We want to reflect what we see as the exceptionally diverse identity of Conservatives across the country – diversity of thought, diversity of experiences and diversity of everything that makes up our society. We are proud of the values that our brand stands for because those values unite people across every walk of life.

WE THE PEOPLE takes things a step further – a portion of the profits from every sale goes directly to supporting causes that reflect the values our community stands for. (They have already given over $250,000 to veterans causes.)

Every sip is another step towards freedom. Drink up!"

Company Name	We The People Wine
CEO	Ryan Coyne
Twitter Handle	@WeThePeopleWine
Instagram Handle	@WeThePeopleWine
Facebook Handle	@WeThePeopleWine
LinkedIn Handle	N/A
YouTube Channel	We The People Wine
Website	**wethepeople.wine**
Industry	Wine
What Makes Them Conservative	They explicitly support conservative values and causes in all they do

62. Charity Mobile

Charity Mobile sends 5% of its customers' monthly plan revenue to the Pro-Life, Pro-Family charity of your choice! Together with their loyal customers, they have sent nearly $2 million dollars to charities so far.

Charity Mobile makes it easy to switch and provides great service and coverage on America's most reliable network! They offer a variety of phones and plans, from easy-to-use flip phones to full-featured smartphones, and monthly data plans that include unlimited talk and unlimited messaging for up to eight lines.

You can help build a Culture of Life in America with every call! They love to do business with like-minded people!

Company Name	Charity Mobile
CEO	Patrick Adams
Twitter Handle	@CharityMobileUS
Instagram Handle	@charitymobileus
Facebook Handle	@charitymobile
LinkedIn Handle	N/A
YouTube Channel	N/A
Website	**charitymobile.com**
Industry	Telecom
What Makes Them Conservative	Sends 5% of the money its users pay to pro-life, pro-family charities.

63. **Sturm, Ruger & Company**

Sturm, Ruger & Company, Inc., better known by the shortened name Ruger, is an American firearm manufacturing company based in Southport, Connecticut, with production facilities also in Newport, New Hampshire; Mayodan, North Carolina; and Prescott, Arizona. The company was founded in 1949 by Alexander McCormick Sturm and William B. Ruger and has been publicly traded on the NYSE since 1969.

Ruger produces bolt-action, semi-automatic, and single-shot rifles, shotguns, semi-automatic pistols, and single-action and double-action revolvers. According to the ATF statistics for 2015, Ruger is currently America's largest firearm manufacturer, as well as the second largest pistol and revolver manufacturer (behind Smith & Wesson) and rifle manufacturer (behind Remington) in the United States.

A gun company that is a fierce defender of the 2nd Amendment, Sturm, Ruger & Co deserves your support.

Company Name	Sturm, Ruger & Company
CEO	Christopher J. Killoy
Twitter Handle	N/A
Instagram Handle	@rugersofficial
Facebook Handle	@Ruger
LinkedIn Handle	/company/ruger-firearms/
YouTube Channel	RugerFirearms
Website	**ruger.com**
Stock Symbol	**RGR (NYSE)**
Industry	Gun Maker
What Makes Them Conservative	Defender of the 2nd Amendment

64. Patriot Mobile

Patriot Mobile is America's Christian conservative wireless service provider. They offer broad coverage on dependable, nationwide 4G or 5G networks. They are committed to providing their members with dependable wireless service and exceptional support, while relentlessly fighting for our shared values. While you're out and about, Patriot Mobile donates a portion of every dollar earned to support organizations that fight for First Amendment Religious Freedom and Freedom of Speech, Second Amendment Right to Bear Arms, Sanctity of Life and the needs of our Veterans and First Responders. Will you partner with them today?

Among the many conservative groups they support are Turning Point USA, the NRA, Council For Life, and Folds Of Honor. The Patriot Mobile Action (PMA) is a non-profit Super PAC and GPAC formed in 2022 and separate from Patriot Mobile LLC. The goal? To SAVE AMERICA. PMA's launch included 11 school board victories and PMA worked hard to keep Texas red in the 2022 General Election. From the Court House to the White House, PMA is fighting for Christian conservative principles.

This company deserves your support. Dump the conventional cell phone providers and go with these guys!

Company Name	Patriot Mobile
CEO	Ron Montgomery
Twitter Handle	@PatriotMobile
Instagram Handle	@PatriotMobileUSA
Facebook Handle	@PatriotMobileUSA
LinkedIn Handle	company/patriotmobile
YouTube Channel	@PatriotMobile
Website	**patriotmobile.com**
Industry	Wireless Phones
What Makes Them Conservative	Everything!!

65. Abt Electronics

Abt was founded in 1936 when Jewel Abt gave her husband David $800 to start a business. Abt began as a small store with only three employees in the Logan Square neighborhood of Chicago. Abt has since grown to become one of the country's largest independent single-store appliance and electronics retailers, situated on 75 acres in Glenview, IL, and employing a staff of more than 1,600 trained experts. Annual revenues are $12.4 Billion.

Abt is a rare company that refuses to kowtow to ESG or other woke nonsense. They deserve your support!!

Company Name	Abt Electronics
CEO	Jon & Mike Abt
Twitter Handle	@AbtElectronics
Instagram Handle	@AbtElectronics
Facebook Handle	@AbtElectronics
LinkedIn Handle	/company/ABTelectronics
YouTube Channel	Abt Electronics
Website	**abt.com**
Industry	Electronics Retail
What Makes Them Conservative	Avoid Wokism. Stand Up for traditional conservative values

66. ADT

ADT Inc. is an American company that provides residential, small and large business electronic security, fire protection, and other related alarm monitoring services throughout the United States. Their corporate head office is in Boca Raton, Florida. They are one of Sean Hannity's top advertisers on his daily TV show on Fox. They have withstood the onslaught of far-left pressure groups like Media Matters to encourage a customer boycott and continued to support his show and the conservative worldview.

Company Name	**ADT**
CEO	Jim DeVries
Twitter Handle	@ADT
Instagram Handle	@adtsecurity
Facebook Handle	@ADT
LinkedIn Handle	/company/adt/
YouTube Channel	ADT
Website	**add.com**
Stock Symbol	**ADT (NYSE)**
Industry	Security Company
What Makes Them Conservative	Advertises on Sean Hannity Show, subject to liberal boycott

67. Remington

Remington is one of the oldest ammunition makers in the United States. They have been around for over 200 years. "Together, Remington and America have fought and won wars, put food on millions of tables, and brought countless generations together at the range and in the field. We are proud of each round that rolls off our factory line. Bringing a renewed focus to ammunition, innovation, and quality, we are reinvigorating our company so you can continue to trust our brand and products – all while staying true to Remington's legendary heritage and stature as an American icon."

Remington is a non-woke, non-ESG, pro-USA company. That's the type of company you want to support, and you want to buy products from.

If you are a conservative, a patriot, and a believer in the 2nd Amendment, then you should own guns and buy ammo. And some of that ammo should be Remington ammo.

Company Name	Remington
CEO	Jacob Wells & Heather Wilson
Twitter Handle	@RemingtonArms
Instagram Handle	@Remington1816
Facebook Handle	@Remington1816
LinkedIn Handle	/company/Remington-Ammunition
YouTube Channel	Remington 1816
Website	**remington.com**
Industry	Guns & Ammo
What Makes Them Conservative	They are a staunch supporter of the 2nd Amendment

68. Salem Media

"Salem Media Group is America's leading radio broadcaster, Internet content provider, and magazine and book publisher targeting audiences interested in Christian and family-themed content and conservative values. In addition to its radio properties, Salem owns Salem Radio Network, which syndicates talk, news and music programming to 3000 affiliates; Salem Radio Representatives, a national radio advertising sales force; Salem Web Network, a leading Internet provider of Christian content and online streaming; and Salem Publishing, a leading publisher of Christian and conservative themed books and magazines. Salem owns and operates 99 radio stations, with 56 stations in the nation's top 25 top markets – and 28 stations in the top 10 markets."

The company was founded in 1974, is publicly traded and has over 1200 employees and $300 million a year in revenue. They are publicly traded on the NASDAQ, and their stock ticker symbol is SALM.

Wayne is a Salem TV host!

They deserve your support!

Company Name	Salem Media
CEO	Dave Santrella
Twitter Handle	@SalemMediaGrp
Instagram Handle	@Salem_Media_Group
Facebook Handle	@SalemMediaGroup
LinkedIn Handle	/company/SalemMediaGroup
YouTube Channel	Salem Media Group Videos
Website	**salemmedia.com**
Stock Symbol	**SALM Class A (NASDAQ)**
Industry	Media & Publishing Company
What Makes Them Conservative	Their platform features the top conservative talkers in America. Salem is a staunch supporter of the 2nd Amendment

69. D. G. Yuengling & Son

D. G. Yuengling & Son is the oldest brewing company in America, established in 1829. By 2018, it was the largest craft brewery, sixth largest overall brewery, and largest wholly American-owned brewery in the United States. Its headquarters are in Pottsville, Pennsylvania. In 2015, Yuengling produced about 2.9 million barrels.

Yuengling is an Anglicized version of Jüngling, its founder's surname and the German term for a "young person" or "youngster".

CEO Dick Yuengling endorsed Donald Trump for President in 2016 and has praised former Governor Tom Corbett for making Pennsylvania a Right-To-Work state.

This is a no-brainer! Stop buying beer from woke companies and start buying beer from Yuengling!

Company Name	D. G. Yuengling & Son
CEO	Dick Yuengling
Twitter Handle	@YuenglingBeer
Instagram Handle	@YuenglingBeer
Facebook Handle	@YuenglingBeer
LinkedIn Handle	/company/d-g-yuengling-&-son-inc/
YouTube Channel	DGYuenglingSon
Website	**yeungling.com**
Industry	Beer
What Makes Them Conservative	Non-woke! America's Oldest Brewery

70. Bassett Furniture

Bassett Furniture Industries is a furniture manufacturer and retailer, headquartered in Bassett, Virginia. It was founded in 1902, by
John D. Bassett, Charles C. Bassett, Samuel H. Bassett, and Reed L.
Stone. Bassett Furniture is one of the oldest furniture manufacturers
in Virginia. Bassett operates 100 retail locations in the United States
and Puerto Rico. They are publicly traded on the NASDAQ. Bassett
strongly supports veterans and first responders and does no woke or
ESG pandering. They make great furniture that lasts, and they deserve
your support!

Company Name	Bassett Furniture
CEO	Robert Spilman, Jr.
Twitter Handle	@BassettUS
Instagram Handle	@BassettFurniture
Facebook Handle	@BassettFurnitureUS
LinkedIn Handle	/company/ bassett-furniture-industries/
YouTube Channel	Bassett Furniture
Website	**bassettfurniture.com**
Stock Symbol	**BSET (NASDAQ)**
Industry	Furniture
What Makes Them Conservative	Non-woke Furniture maker based in Virginia

Proudly Patriotic

This next group of companies are all proudly patriotic and embrace the Bill Of Rights in their DNA. They love America and believe in its promise. Their business is a love letter to America and the patriots who built her. They deserve your support.

71. Daniel Defense

"Daniel Defense is a family-owned and privately held firearms manufacturer located in Black Creek, Georgia. Founded in 2000 by President/CEO Marty Daniel, the company was born from Marty's vision to create custom rifle accessories for his personal rifles. Eighteen years later, Daniel's concepts have evolved into one of the most recognizable brands in the firearms world, consisting of the world's finest AR15-style rifles, pistols, bolt-action rifles, and accessories for civilian, law enforcement, and military customers. At Daniel Defense, **we celebrate the liberty of our country**, the enthusiasm of our customers and employees, and the quality and accuracy of our products."

That is all you need to know to support this great company!!!

Company Name	Daniel Defense
CEO	Marty Daniel
Twitter Handle	@DanielDefense
Instagram Handle	@DanielDefense
Facebook Handle	@DanielDefense
LinkedIn Handle	/company/daniel-defense-inc./
YouTube Channel	DanielDefense
Website	**danieldefense.com**
Industry	Guns, Outdoor and Sporting Goods
What Makes Them Conservative	Pro-2nd Amendment and fights to protect our right to keep and bear arms

72. Anheuser-Busch

Anheuser-Busch is the largest alcoholic beverage company on the planet. It is most famous for its Budweiser brand of beer, among several others.

One of the largest shareholders of Anheuser-Busch is the Anheuser Family. As with many other rich German families, they are extremely private, with a limited role in politics, although it is well-known that they are conservative. They are a subsidiary of a public company, AB InBev, which owns many major beer brands.

Anheuser-Busch executives and shareholders donated over $60,000 to Republican and conservative campaigns in 2020. They have also organized several PACs to donate money to Republican campaigns.

They aren't woke, and they don't toe the ESG line. Their CEO is an ex-Marine and CIA operative, from back when those folks were real patriots. Hoist up a Bud!

Company Name	Anheuser-Busch
CEO	Brendan Whitworth
Twitter Handle	@AnheuserBusch
Instagram Handle	@AnheuserBusch
Facebook Handle	@AnheuserBusch
LinkedIn Handle	/company/anheuser-busch
YouTube Channel	Anheuser-Busch
Website	**Anheuser-Busch.com**
Stock Symbol	**BUD (NYSE)**
Industry	Brewery
What Makes Them Conservative	Supports Republican Causes and Candidates

73. Publix

Publix is one of the world's largest privately-owned supermarkets, with over $41 billion in annual revenues. In an era where most other supermarkets have become more liberal, Publix has become more conservative. Where most other supermarkets have doubled down on "No gun" policies, Publix has publicly stated it doesn't really mind legal conceal and carry in their stores, if it is for self-defense reasons.

The Jenkins and Barnett families (who own the largest shares in Publix) are both very private families. However, both are known to be very conservative fiscally, donating millions of dollars every year to conservative causes and candidates. In recent years, Publix has made headlines for its record donations to Republican campaigns, and to Governor Ron DeSantis, America's Best Governor™. During the 2020 Presidential Campaign, Publix executives and shareholders contributed over $50,000 to Republican candidates. They have donated over $100,000 to Governor DeSantis.

Order your groceries from Publix!

Company Name	Publix
CEO	Todd Jones
Twitter Handle	@Publix
Instagram Handle	@Publix
Facebook Handle	@Publix
LinkedIn Handle	/company/Publix
YouTube Channel	Publix
Website	**publix.com**
Industry	Grocery Chain
What Makes Them Conservative	Supports Republican Causes and Candidates, including Governor Ron DeSantis, America's Best Governor

74. Exxon-Mobil

Exxon-Mobil is one of the largest oil and natural gas companies, with $280 billion a year in revenue. Since the 1980s, Exxon-Mobil, alongside several other oil companies, has slowly been donating more and more to Republican candidates.

Since the 1980s, the Democratic party, in the grip of its Marxist and anti-oil wing, has been demonizing and attempting to destroy the industry.

As a result, Exxon-Mobil and other oil companies have supported Republican candidates, donating millions in recent years. They are publicly traded on the NYSE.

Fill up at an Exxon or Mobil station!

Company Name	Exxon-Mobil
CEO	Darren Woods
Twitter Handle	@ExxonMobil
Instagram Handle	@ExxonMobil
Facebook Handle	@ExxonMobil
LinkedIn Handle	/company/ExxonMobil
YouTube Channel	ExxonMobil
Website	**corporate.exxonmobil.com**
Stock Symbol	XOM (NYSE)
Industry	Energy Company
What Makes Them Conservative	Supports Republican Causes and Candidates

75. Duck Commander

As one of the only shows portraying a traditional, conservative, Christian family, **Duck Dynasty** put Duck Commander on the map. Phil Robertson, the family patriarch, who is a deeply committed Christian and conservative, founded the company. He endorsed and campaigned for Senator Ted Cruz in the 2016 election, while his son and the company's CEO, Willie, did the same for the eventual winner, President Donald Trump. Phil became one of Trump's biggest supporters after his election and has spoken out publicly against the evils of the woke and anti-faith hatred being promoted by the vicious Left. The Robertsons are an altogether wonderful family and stalwarts of traditional American values. Their books are also incredibly funny and easy to read.

Buy their gear! Read their books! And hire them to speak for your company events!

Company Name	Duck Commander
CEO	Willie Roberston
Twitter Handle	@Duck_Commander
Instagram Handle	@OfficialDuckCommander
Facebook Handle	@OfficialDuckCommander
LinkedIn Handle	/company/Duck-Commander
YouTube Channel	Duck Commander
Website	**duckcommander.com**
Industry	Hunting Gear
What Makes Them Conservative	Traditional American Company, famous for their love of America and stand for her and all that makes her great

76. Parler

Parler became famous when they rose dramatically up the App store rankings after Twitter banned President Trump, and conservatives revolted by abandoning the formerly woke platform in droves. They were created as a space that allows free speech and does not cancel conservatives. CEO George Farmer is the husband of conservative firebrand Candace Owens.

They have a great platform and are worthy of your support!

Company Name	Parler
CEO	George Farmer
Twitter Handle	@parler_app
Instagram Handle	@parler_app
Facebook Handle	Proudly Suspended from Facebook
LinkedIn Handle	/company/parlerinc/
YouTube Channel	Parler
Website	**parler.com**
Industry	Social Networking
What Makes Them Conservative	Supports free speech and Conservatism

77. PetSmart

PetSmart is a privately held American chain of pet superstores founded in 1986 by Jim and Janice Dougherty, which sells pet products, services, and small pets. It is the leading North American pet company, and its indirect competitors are Amazon, Walmart, and Target. As of 2020, PetSmart has more than 1,650 stores in the United States, Canada, and Puerto Rico. Its stores sell pet food, pet supplies, pet accessories, and small pets. Stores also provide services including grooming, dog daycare, dog and cat boarding, veterinary care via in-store third-party clinics, and dog training. They also offer dog and cat adoption via in-store adoption centers, facilitated by the nonprofit PetSmart Charities. They deserve your support!

Company Name	Petsmart
CEO	J.K Symancyk
Twitter Handle	@PetSmart
Instagram Handle	@PetSmart
Facebook Handle	@PetSmart
LinkedIn Handle	/company/petsmart/
YouTube Channel	PetSmart
YouTube Channel	**PetSmart.com**
Industry	Superstore For Pet Products
What Makes Them Conservative	Conservative company and supports conservative causes

78. **South State Bank**

South State Bank, based in Winter Haven, Florida, is a subsidiary of South State Corporation, a bank holding company. The company has 300 branches in Florida, South Carolina, North Carolina, Georgia, and Virginia. The bank has $34 billion in assets. It is publicly traded on the NASDAQ, with the stock ticker symbol SSB. Like many conservative companies, its activities are primarily in red states! They deserve your support!

Company Name	South State Bank
CEO	Robert R. Hill Jr
Twitter Handle	@SouthStateBank
Instagram Handle	@SouthStateBank
Facebook Handle	@SouthStateBank
LinkedIn Handle	company/south-state-bank/
YouTube Channel	SouthState Bank
Website	**southstatebank.com**
Stock Symbol	**SSB (NASDAQ)**
Industry	Financial Services
What Makes Them Conservative	98% of donations go to Conservative causes

79. FrankSpeech.com

Lindell TV is part of Mike Lindell's FrankSpeech free speech platform, where he seeks to promote free speech and the principles of the constitutional Republic! Lindell TV features many great leaders and stars of the conservative movement including Mike Lindell, Steve Bannon, Brannon Howse, Roger Stone, Emerald Robinson, and the co-author of this book, Wayne Allyn Root.

Here is a lengthy, direct quote from the FrankSpeech website:

"The Community Standards for Frank Are Based Upon America's Constitutional Republic and the Laws of Nature and Nature's God That Are Its Foundation.

America's Founding Fathers established America as a Constitutional Republic that is specifically based on the Ten Commandments and the law of nature and nature's God. One need only visit the Jefferson Memorial in Washington, DC and read the inscriptions on its walls to understand the fundamental role God has played in guiding our Republic. As Thomas Jefferson stated, "God, who gave us life, gave us liberty. Can the liberties of a nation be secure when we have removed a conviction that these liberties are the gift of God?"

In keeping with that belief, FrankSpeech is a place for discussion by those who recognize our freedoms are gifts, not from government, but from God. Currently, Big Tech and the mainstream media are censoring individuals who speak out on events that are undermining our Republic and transgressing on our God given rights. FrankSpeech is a forum for discussing these issues free from their censorship."

Company Name	FrankSpeech.com
CEO	Mike Lindell
Twitter Handle	@TheRealFrankSp1
Instagram Handle	N/A
Facebook Handle	N/A
LinkedIn Handle	N/A
YouTube Channel	N/A
Website	**frankspeech.com**
Industry	Media Company & Platform
What Makes Them Conservative	Mike Lindell's Media Company. Features author Wayne Allyn Root's TV show daily at 7 PM ET on Lindell 2 and repeated daily at 4 PM ET on Lindell 1.

80. Twitter

Twitter was one of the worst of the worst woke companies, and they may well be guilty of electoral malfeasance, whereby they threw the election to Joe Biden by actively coordinating with the FBI, DNC and the Biden campaign during the 2020 election, to censor the Hunter Biden laptop story and gaslight, censor, suspend and ban conservatives who attempted to cry foul (including co-author Wayne Allyn Root, who was banned in early 2021). But now that Twitter has been bought by Elon Musk, and he has reinstated President Trump's account, as well as other great conservatives like Jordan Peterson and actor James Woods, given a general amnesty to all suspended accounts, and released the bombshell internal memos and emails outlining the coordination between the FBI, Twitter and the DNC to censor conservatives, Twitter is now a company that deserves your support!

Company Name	Twitter
CEO	Elon Musk
Twitter Handle	@Twitter
Instagram Handle	@Twitter
Facebook Handle	@TwitterInc
LinkedIn Handle	/company/twitter/
YouTube Channel	Twitter
Website	**twitter.com**
Industry	Social Media App
What Makes Them Conservative	Reinstated Trump and Conservatives, Blew The Whistle on DNC & Twitter Collusion

81. Red Rock Resorts/Station Casinos

Red Rock Resorts/Station Casinos, LLC is an American hotel and casino company based in Summerlin, a suburb of Las Vegas. Frank Fertitta, Jr. founded the company as Station Casinos. Red Rock Resorts is the holding company that is publicly traded, but Stations Casinos is the brand that most people are familiar with. Red Rock Resorts owns Station Casinos, along with Affinity Gaming, Boyd Gaming and Golden Entertainment, and they dominate the locals' casino market in Las Vegas. Station Casinos has also branched out into managing casinos that they do not own. Their revenues are $1.4 billion a year, and they employ 11,000 people.

Run by the founder's son, Frank Fertitta III, Station is a major donor to the Republican Party, and supports conservative causes. They deserve your support. If you enjoy gambling, and live in Las Vegas, or are visiting, spend your money at Station Casinos! Their biggest, boldest, most high-profile, upscale mega-casinos are the Red Rock Resort in Summerlin and Green Valley Ranch Resort in Henderson.

Company Name	Red Rock Resorts/Station Casinos
CEO	Frank Fertitta III
Twitter Handle	@stationcasinos
Instagram Handle	@stationcasinos
Facebook Handle	@stationcasinos
LinkedIn Handle	/company/station-casinos/
YouTube Channel	StationCasinos
Website	**redrockresorts.com**
Stock Symbol	**RRR (NASDAQ)**
Industry	Gambling & Gaming Company
What Makes Them Conservative	Donate money to Republicans and conservative causes

82. The Gateway Pundit

The Gateway Pundit was founded by Jim Hoft just prior to the 2004 United States presidential election, to speak the truth and to expose the evil of the Left. The website's name refers to the Gateway Arch in the city of St. Louis, Missouri, where Hoft lives.

In 2016, The Gateway Pundit was one of the few mainstream media sites that provided accurate and unbiased coverage of Donald Trump's presidential campaign. After Trump's victory, TGP was granted press credentials by the White House. A 2017 study found that The Gateway Pundit was the fourth most-shared source among Trump supporters on Twitter during the 2016 election, behind Fox News, The Hill and Breitbart News.

They were proudly banned by the former owners of Twitter (on the same day as coauthor Wayne Allyn Root), for bravely standing up to the leftwing censor machine that ran that site.

You can trust the news stories at The Gateway Pundit, and you should support them.

Company Name	The Gateway Pundit
CEO	Jim Hoft
Twitter Handle	Proudly suspended by Twitter
Instagram Handle	@gatewaypundit
Facebook Handle	@gatewaypundit
LinkedIn Handle	N/A
YouTube Channel	@GatewayPunditVideo
Website	thegatewaypundit.com
Industry	Media Company
What Makes Them Conservative	Conservative Media Company, Pro-Trump & Pro-Freedom

83. Zero Hedge

Launched in 2009, Zero Hedge is a finance blog that presents both in-house analysis and analysis from investment banks, hedge funds, and other investment writers and analysts. Zero Hedge adheres to the free-market Austrian School of Economics and has a mission to "widen the scope of financial, economic and political information available to the professional investing public".

One of the interesting elements of this website is that there are several contributors that write for it, and they all use the pseudonym "Tyler Durden" who is a character from the film the Fight Club. They don't want to be doxxed and attacked by the evil Left.

Zero Hedge is deeply committed to freedom and pure capitalism (as opposed to crony capitalism) and is very pro-traditional U.S. values. They deserve your support.

Company Name	Zero Hedge
Founder & Main Editor	"Tyler Durden" rumored to actually be Daniel Ivandjiiski
Twitter Handle	@zerohedge
Instagram Handle	N/A
Facebook Handle	N/A
LinkedIn Handle	N/A
YouTube Channel	@zerohedge9531
Website	**zerohedge.com**
Industry	Media Company
What Makes Them Conservative	Libertarian Media Company, anti-socialist, anti-woke, anti-crony capitalism, pro freedom and pure capitalism

84. The Liberty Daily

The Liberty Daily is the conservative alternative to The Drudge Report. It's pro-conservative, pro-Christian, and fearless. It is owned and operated by Matthew & Jennifer Burke.

Here is what founder Matt Burke has to say about the site: "My wife Jennifer and I started The Liberty Daily in 2015 as a conservative alternative to Drudge, which I felt needed some competition. I was frustrated by the amount of traffic he was driving to left-wing publications like the New York Times and Washington Post. Plus, he wasn't doing anything to help conservatives in the culture wars which we've been getting clobbered on by the Left for decades."

Here is a direct quote from Burke that we love: "I don't get caught up in trying to post links to stories that get the most clicks, unlike most websites. I want to put up stories that are pro-Christian, pro-Constitution, pro-America, anti-Communism and try to fight the evil forces that are trying to destroy America through the culture."

The site, which started out around 50 views per month and continues to grow beyond its current level of 2 million visitors per month, has no problem calling things the way they should be seen. Unlike "polite" news aggregators and opinion sources, The Liberty Daily is bold in the way they present the news without going down the road of hysteria or hyperbole.

When asked "What does America need the most, in one sentence?" He didn't need a sentence. He didn't even need a phrase. He summed it up in one word. "Jesus." And he's right!

We agree with Matt wholeheartedly and encourage you to drop Drudge and start visiting the Liberty Daily.

Company Name	The Liberty Daily
CEO	Matt Burke
Twitter Handle	@TheLibertyDaily
Instagram Handle	N/A
Facebook Handle	N/A
LinkedIn Handle	N/A
YouTube Channel	@ThePoliStick
Website	**thelibertydaily.com**
Industry	Media Company
What Makes Them Conservative	Conservative, Christian Media Company, anti-socialist and anti-woke

85. Natural News

Natural News is a website that opposes Big Pharma propaganda and censorship, Covid vaccination lies, and GMOs (among many other threats to our health). Their TV and radio podcasts on Brighteon are largely conservative content.

Natural News has accurately noted numerous times that Ivermectin and Vitamin D3 (among many other vitamins and nutrients) are safe and effective to build your immune system and protect against illness and disease. They have huge traffic at NaturalNews.com—over 7 million unique visitors a month. The far-left hates them, and Wikipedia constantly smears them as "far-right", which in our view, means "so far, they're right about everything."

They are a great site, and you should absolutely visit them and share their content! Not just at NaturalNews.com, but on brighteon.tv and brighteonradio.com. One of the many fantastic shows they carry is "Wayne Allyn Root: Raw & Unfiltered."

Company Name	Natural News
CEO	Mike Adams
Twitter Handle	@NaturalNews01
Instagram Handle	N/A
Facebook Handle	N/A
LinkedIn Handle	N/A
YouTube Channel	@NaturalNews
Website	naturalnews.com
Industry	Media Company, Brighteon. tv, Brighteonradio.com
What Makes Them Conservative	Libertarian, conservative, pro-health, holistic, natural health, pro-personal responsibility and anti-Big Pharma

86. Cornerstone Payment Systems

Cornerstone is one of the nation's leading Christian-owned and operated independent sales organizations in the merchant processing industry. They have a commitment to separate their transaction processing services from the remainder of the industry. They do this by putting Christ at the cornerstone of their business. As a part of their commitment, they will not process credit card transactions for what they believe are morally objectionable businesses. In other words, they will not do business with organizations that promote left ideologies at the center of their business mission. They boldly state that they are blessed to serve leading ministries and businesses across the US. They are a great alternative to payment processors that have capitulated to wokism.

Company Name	Cornerstone Payment Systems
CEO	Nick Logan
Twitter Handle	@CornerstonePay
Instagram Handle	@cornerstonepays
Facebook Handle	@cornerstonepays
LinkedIn Handle	/company/cornerstone-west-payment-systems/
YouTube Channel	N/A
Website	CornerstonePaymentSystems.com
Industry	Finance
What Makes Them Conservative	Christian Payment Processor

87. Silver State Radio

Silver State Radio is the company founded and owned by Wayne Allyn Root, co-author of this book. Silver State Radio produces the properties and brands of conservative media superstar Wayne Allyn Root—nationally-syndicated radio show, Las Vegas radio show, national TV shows on Lindell TV and Real America's Voice TV Network, podcasts, newspaper commentaries, books and the website ROOTforAmerica.com.

How can you support Wayne and his conservative brand? Silver State Radio sells advertising and sponsorships on all of Wayne's media properties and platforms. If you own a business—small, medium, or large—it's a WIN-WIN for everyone if you advertise with Wayne, or sponsor one of his shows.

You are supporting Wayne so he can keep fighting and defending America, American exceptionalism and capitalism.

And your company or product will be exposed to a large audience of consumers with disposable incomes (conservatives buy 60% of all products in America) who want to buy products associated with Wayne, used by Wayne, and endorsed by Wayne.

Wayne also speaks at events around the USA about business, politics, capitalism, and his famous "TRUMP RULES." Wayne speaks at corporations, conventions, conferences, Republican clubs and events, and college Republican events. Contact Silver State Radio to discuss speaking engagements, advertising, or sponsorships.

Company Name	Silver State Radio
CEO	Wayne Allyn Root
Parler Handle	@RealWayneRoot
GETTR Handle	@WayneRoot
Truth Social Handle	@RealWayneRoot
Website	**RootForAmerica.com**
Email	WayneRoot@gmail.com
Industry	TV and radio shows, podcasts, books, speeches, newspaper columns
What Makes Them Conservative	Wayne Allyn Root's Company!!

88. eCircle Academy

eCircle Inc, operating as eCircle Academy (**www.eCircleAcademy.com**), is Nicky Billou's company, co-author of this book. They run workshops, masterminds and programs for Coaches, Consultants, Corporate Trainers, Clinic Owners, Realtors, Mortgage Brokers and other service-based Entrepreneurs, to help them grow their businesses, by positioning them as thought leaders and authorities in their niche. The heart of eCircle's business is their belief in God, Jesus, the Constitution, freedom, free expression & free enterprise.

Many service-based entrepreneurs, especially those under $1 million in sales, are very good at doing the technical work in their business, but they are not trained businesspeople. They don't understand sales & marketing, profit & loss statements, hiring & firing, culture, systems and processes and many other aspects of running an actual business. Nicky and his team help these companies turn their passion into a thriving business, with 1 to 2 zeroes added to their annual income.

They also provide business coaching, book ghost-writing, podcast guest training and podcast launch training services for their clients.

They have recently launched a new program for CEOs of established companies, helping turn them into the Elon Musk or Patrick Bet-David of their space, so that they are seen as a branded CEO, and can help drive the growth and scaling of their business. eCircle reflects the deeply Christian and conservative values of its founders and works with Christian and conservative business owners to help them win. If you are a Christian, you don't have to work with business advisors and coaches who don't share your values. You should never have to compromise your values to grow your business.

How can you support Nicky and his conservative brand? If you own a business—small, medium, or large —and you need help growing it, it's a WIN-WIN for everyone if you engage Nicky and his team to help you do it.

Company Name	eCircle Academy
CEO	Nicky Billou
Twitter Handle	@NickyBillou
Instagram Handle	@NickyBillou
Facebook Handle	@NickyBillou
LinkedIn Handle	/company/NickyBillou/
YouTube Channel	NickyBillou
Website	**eCircleAcademy.com**
Email	nicky@ecircle.ca
Industry	Business Workshops, Coaching
What Makes Them Conservative	Nicky Billou's Company!!!!

89. Nevada Corporate Headquarters

Nevada Corporate Headquarters, Inc. (NCH) helps American patriots form Nevada Limited Liability Companies (LLCs) to safely store their money and financial assets. With over 200,000 businesses formed, NCH provides a variety of services for American businesses to assist them in legally protecting themselves from personal liability, lawsuits, and government overreach, while providing financial anonymity from prying eyes. If you're an American business owner, a real estate investor, or someone who has assets to protect, a Nevada Limited Liability Company, or LLC, is the best defense against anyone trying to take assets away from you. No matter where you live, you can take advantage of the benefits of a Nevada LLC. The federal government is taking more and more of your hard-earned money. Now is the time to let Nevada's asset protection laws preserve your hard-earned wealth. Form a Nevada LLC and protect what's yours. Visit nchinc.com.

Nevada Corporate Headquarters (NCH) believes in free enterprise, capitalism, and the American Dream.

If you are looking to set up a corporation, and protect your assets, use NCH!

Company Name	Nevada Corporate Headquarters
CEO	Cort Christie
Twitter Handle	@nvcorphqtrs
Instagram Handle	@nchinc
Facebook Handle	N/A
LinkedIn Handle	/company/KipHerriage
YouTube Channel	NVCorpHqtrs
Website	**NevadaWAR.com**
Industry	Investing
What Makes Them Conservative	Founder is a committed free market Conservative; they advertise on conservative media

90. Vertical Research Advisory

Vertical Research Advisory, LLC is a top-performing daily Investment & Economic Advisory that was founded by Kip Herriage. The VRA Portfolio has outperformed the broad markets in 16 out of the 19 years since inception. After leaving behind his 15-year career on Wall Street in 1999, where Kip took 7 companies public and raised hundreds of millions of dollars, Kip started the VRA in 2003, which he publishes daily for subscribers around the world (including Wayne Allyn Root—coauthor of this book). Wayne wakes up every morning to read his latest VRA edition. The newsletter website is VRAinsider.com.

Kip and his oldest son/partner Tyler, are 5th and 6th generation native Texans and are proud "red-pilled American Patriots."

Come join the smart money at the VRA.

Company Name	Vertical Research Advisory, LLC
CEO	Kip Herriage
TruthSocial Handle	@kipherriage
GETTR Handle	@kipherriage
Facebook Handle	@nchinc
LinkedIn Handle	/company/ nevada-corporate-headquarters
YouTube Channel	Vertical Research Advisory
Website	VRAInsider.com
Industry	Investment Advice
What Makes Them Conservative	5th Generation Red-Pilled Native Texan. MAGA!

91. Fox News Channel

Fox is the biggest cable news network in America. It features some amazingly balanced and right-leaning shows, and conservative superstars like Tucker Carlson, Jesse Watters, Greg Gutfeld, Judge Jeanine Pirro, Sean Hannity, Mark Levin, Dan Bongino, and Laura Ingram (among others). However, they are moving more left and anti-Trump. They refused to allow straight talk on either stolen elections or vaccine mandates. Paul Ryan on their Board is a vicious anti-Trumper. There are problems at FNC. But they remain the highest-rated channel for conservative viewers. We will keep an eye on FNC, but for now, no conservative list can be complete without them. They are a subsidiary of Fox Corporation, which is publicly traded on the NASDAQ.

Company Name	Fox News Channel
CEO	Suzanne Scott
Truth Handle	@FoxNews
GETTR Handle	@FoxNews
Facebook Handle	@FoxNews
LinkedIn Handle	/company/fox-news-channel/
YouTube Channel	Fox News
Website	**foxnews.com**
Stock Symbol	**FOXA (NASDAQ)**
Industry	Media
What Makes Them Conservative	Offers Conservative and fair news reporting

92. Newsmax

Newsmax Media is a conservative news and media company. It is far more conservative than the Fox News Channel.

They publish a monthly magazine, maintain a website, and offer a cable television channel, NewsMax TV. They also send out daily emails of breaking news stories of interest that may not be fully covered in the general media. Newsmax was founded to point out liberal bias and improprieties in the media that are forced upon the American people, and they report true news. They also seek to extol men and women who show conservative virtues.

Newsmax is a great company and deserves your support!

Company Name	Newsmax
CEO	Chris Ruddy
Truth Handle	@Newsmax
GETTR Handle	@Newsmax
Facebook Handle	@Newsmax
LinkedIn Handle	/company/newsmax-media-inc-/
YouTube Channel	NewsmaxTV
Website	**newsmax.com**
Industry	Media
What Makes Them Conservative	Newsmax has Conservative and fair news reporting

93. WINNERS Inc./VegasWINNERS Inc.

VegasWinners.com is an online sports gaming information company founded and headed by co-author Wayne Allyn Root. The company is owned by parent company WINNERS Inc. which is publicly traded (Ticker Symbol: WNRS). Wayne is the single largest shareholder of the public company.

Sports gaming has been called, "America's new national past-time." Wayne himself has been dubbed by the media, "America's Oddsmaker" and "the King of Vegas Sports Gaming." Wayne is the only sports gaming personality in the world with a 180-pound granite star on the Las Vegas Walk of Stars.

Billions of dollars a year are wagered on sports. Sports gaming is now legal in 35 states plus Washington DC (on the way to what experts predict will eventually be 44 states). Tens of millions of Americans wager on sports—overwhelmingly men. And those men and women tend to support personal and economic freedom and capitalism (i.e. they're predominantly Republican-conservative).

VegasWINNERS.com provides advice, analysis, research and predictions for sports bettors. Just like MyPillow.com or GreatPatriotStore.com, if you're going to wager on any sports event, and you desire quality investment advice, choose to buy from a company run by a great American conservative and patriot (CEO Wayne Allyn Root).

Company Name	Winners Inc.
CEO	Wayne Allyn Root
Twitter Handle	@VegasWinnersInc
Instagram Handle	N/A
Facebook Handle	N/A
LinkedIn Handle	N/A
YouTube Channel	N/A
Website	**VegasWinners.com**
Stock Symbol	**WNRS (OTC PINK)**
Industry	Sports Betting
What Makes Them Conservative	Company run by a conservative patriot, co-author Wayne Allyn Root!

94. Marriott International Inc.

Marriott International, Inc. is an American hotel, residential and timeshare company headquartered in Bethesda, Maryland. The company was founded by J. Willard Marriott and his wife Alice Marriott, both staunch conservative Mormons. They are the largest hotel company in the world, and the Marriott family remains one of the most pro-American and conservative founding families of any major corporation in America.

The company takes a strong stand against human trafficking, which very few companies have had the courage to do.

The family is still very much involved in running the company, and they are publicly traded on the NASDAQ with the stock symbol MAR. They deserve your support! Stay at their properties and consider investing in their stock!

Company Name	Marriott International
CEO	Anthony Capuano
Twitter Handle	@marriottintl
Instagram Handle	@marriottintl
Facebook Handle	@marriottinternational
LinkedIn Handle	company/marriott-international/
YouTube Channel	MarriottIntl
Website	**marriott.com**
Stock Symbol	MAR (NASADAQ)
Industry	Hotels & Resorts
What Makes Them Conservative	Founding family are deeply conservative Mormons! They take a strong stand against human trafficking

The MAGA Fund

The MAGA Fund is an ETF that was created to push back against the ESG, woketard trend in corporate and to promote companies that support American values with their dollars, in other words, by donating to Republican and Conservative causes. This list includes a select few who primarily give money to Republican politicians and causes. They deserve your support.

95. All State

All State is a large corporation, and with 2021 revenues of $44 billion it ranked 79th in the 2019 Fortune 500 list of the largest United States corporations by total revenue. Its long-running advertising campaign, in use since 1950, asks, "Are you in good hands?", and the recognizable logo portrays a suburban-style dwelling cradled protectively in a pair of giant human hands.

The MAGA Fund, led by Hal Lambert, lists All State as one of the top companies in its portfolio. Their contributions go almost exclusively to Republicans.

You are in good (conservative) hands with All State.

Company Name	All State
CEO	Thomas J. Wilson
Twitter Handle	@AllState
Instagram Handle	@AllState
Facebook Handle	@AllState
LinkedIn Handle	company/allstate
YouTube Channel	@AllState
Website	allstate.com
Stock Symbol	ALL (NYSE)
Industry	Insurance Company
What Makes Them Conservative	Almost All Contributions Go To Republicans

96. J. M. Smucker Company

The J.M. Smucker Company, also known as Smuckers, makes food and beverage products. Headquartered in Orrville, Ohio, the company was founded in 1897 to make apple butter. J.M. Smucker currently has three major business units: consumer foods, pet foods, and coffee. Its flagship brand, Smucker's, produces fruit preserves, peanut butter, syrups, frozen crustless sandwiches, and ice cream toppings. Yum yum!

Among J.M. Smucker's other food and coffee brands are Knott's Berry Farm, Jif, Laura Scudder's, Santa Cruz Organic, Folgers, Café Bustelo, Dunkin', Smucker's Uncrustables, Bick's Pickle, Carnation, Crosse & Blackwell, Eagle Brand, Five Roses, and Robin Hood. Their pet food brands include 9Lives, Gravy Train, Kibbles 'n Bits, Meow Mix, Milk-Bone, and Rachael Ray Nutrish, among others. Listed on the New York Stock Exchange, J.M. Smucker ranks 378th on the Fortune 500, with an estimated 2021 market value of $13.9 billion. They are a Top Holding of the MAGA Fund. They also extensively support veterans causes.

Company Name	J. M. Smucker Company
CEO	Mark Smucker
Twitter Handle	@Smuckers
Instagram Handle	@JMSmuckerCo
Facebook Handle	@Smuckers
LinkedIn Handle	company/the-jm-smucker-co
YouTube Channel	@Smuckers
Website	**jmsmucker.com**
Stock Symbol	**SJM (NYSE)**
Industry	Food & Beverage Company
What Makes Them Conservative	Almost All Contributions Go To Republicans

97. Marathon Petroleum Corporation

Marathon Petroleum Corporation is a petroleum refining, marketing, and transportation company headquartered in Findlay, Ohio. The company was a wholly-owned subsidiary of Marathon Oil until a corporate spin-off in 2011. Following its acquisition of Andeavor on October 1, 2018, Marathon Petroleum became the largest petroleum refinery operator in the United States, with 16 refineries and over 3 million barrels per day of refining capacity. Marathon Petroleum ranked No. 41 on the 2018 Fortune 500 list of the largest United States corporations by total revenue. In the 2020 Forbes Global 2000, Marathon Petroleum was ranked as the 197th-largest public company in the world. They are the #1 company on the MAGA Fund list of holdings.

Company Name	Marathon Petroleum Corporation
CEO	Mike Hennigen
Twitter Handle	@MarathonPetroCo
Instagram Handle	@marathonpetroleum
Facebook Handle	@MarathonPetroleumCorporation
LinkedIn Handle	company/ marathon-petroleum-company
YouTube Channel	@marathonpetroleumcorporati7074
Website	**marathonpetroleum.com**
Stock Symbol	MPC (NYSE)
Industry	Oil & Gas Company
What Makes Them Conservative	Almost All Contributions Go To Republicans

98. FedEx Corporation

FedEx Corporation is an American multinational conglomerate holding company, focused on transportation, e-commerce and business services based in Memphis, Tennessee. FedEx's prominence in both the United States and the world has made it a common topic in popular culture, with examples including the film *Cast Away* as well as some of its marketing slogans (most famously "when it absolutely positively has to be there overnight"). In addition, FedEx has purchased the naming rights to FedExField of the NFL's Washington Commanders and FedExForum of the NBA's Memphis Grizzlies. FedEx's air shipping services have made its main hub (aka the "Superhub") at Memphis International Airport the busiest cargo airport in the world by 2020.

FedEx is the #2 company on the MAGA Fund list! Use them to send your packages!

Company Name	FedEx Corporation
CEO	Raj Subramaniam
Twitter Handle	@FedEx
Instagram Handle	@FedEx
Facebook Handle	@FedExCanada
LinkedIn Handle	company/fedex
YouTube Channel	@FedEx
Website	**fedex.com**
Stock Symbol	**FDX (NYSE)**
Industry	Delivery Company
What Makes Them Conservative	Almost All Contributions Go To Republicans

99. UPS

United Parcel Service (UPS) is an American multinational shipping & receiving and supply chain management company, founded in 1907. UPS has grown to become a Fortune 500 company and one of the world's largest shipping couriers. UPS today is primarily known for its ground shipping services, as well as the UPS Store, a retail chain which assists UPS shipments and provides tools for small businesses. In addition, UPS offers air shipping on an overnight or two-day basis, and delivers to post office boxes through UPS SurePost, a subsidiary that passes on packages to the United States Postal Service for last-mile delivery.

UPS is the largest courier company in the world by revenue, with annual revenues around US$85 billion in 2020. They are not perfect from a conservative point of view, but they do donate heavily to conservative causes and are #5 on the MAGA Fund list.

Company Name	UPS
CEO	Carol Tomé
Twitter Handle	@UPS
Instagram Handle	@UPS
Facebook Handle	@UPS
LinkedIn Handle	company/UPS
YouTube Channel	@UPS
Website	UPS.com
Stock Symbol	UPS Class B (NYSE)
Industry	Courier Company
What Makes Them Conservative	Almost All Contributions Go To Republicans

100. Valero Energy Corporation

Valero Energy Corporation is a Fortune 500 international manufacturer and marketer of transportation fuels, other petrochemical products, and power, headquartered in San Antonio, Texas. Throughout the United States and Canada, the company owns and operates 15 refineries, and one in Wales, with a combined throughput capacity of approximately 3 million barrels (480,000 m3) per day; as well as 11 ethanol plants with a combined production capacity of 1.2 billion US gallons (4,500,000 m3) per year; and a 50-megawatt wind farm. Before the 2013 spinoff of CST Brands, Valero was one of the United States' largest retail operators with approximately 6,800 retail and branded wholesale outlets in the United States, Canada, United Kingdom, and the Caribbean under the Valero, Diamond Shamrock, Shamrock, Beacon, and Texaco brands. They are #6 on the MAGA Fund List.

Company Name	Valero Energy Corporation
CEO	Joseph Gorder
Twitter Handle	@ValeroEnergy
Instagram Handle	@ValeroEnergy
Facebook Handle	@ValeroEnergy
LinkedIn Handle	N/A
YouTube Channel	@ValeroEnergy1
Website	**valero.com**
Stock Symbol	**VLO (NYSE)**
Industry	Oil & Gas Company
What Makes Them Conservative	Almost All Contributions Go To Republicans

101. Home Depot

The Home Depot is an iconic American home improvement company that sells tools, construction products, appliances, and services. Founded by Republican megadonors Bernie Marcus and Ken Langone, Home Depot is the largest home improvement retailer in the United States. In 2021, the company had 490,600 employees and more than $151 billion in revenue. The company is headquartered in Cobb County, Georgia, with an Atlanta mailing address.

Home Depot is a massive donor to Republican and conservative causes, and they are a mainstay of the MAGA Fund!

Company Name	Home Depot
CEO	Craig Menear
Twitter Handle	@HomeDepot
Instagram Handle	@homedepot
Facebook Handle	@TheHomeDepotUSA
LinkedIn Handle	/company/the-home-depot/
YouTube Channel	The Home Depot
Website	**homedepot.com**
Stock Symbol	**HD (NYSE)**
Industry	Home Improvement
What Makes Them Conservative	Doesn't support BLM riots, reliably supports Republican politicians and donated thousands of dollars to conservative candidates

102. **Molson Coors**

Molson Coors was formed in 2005, via the merger of 2 iconic North American brewing companies, Molson and Coors. Coors Vice-Chairman Pete Coors and his family have a long-standing history of supporting freedom, free enterprise and limited government. Pete was the 2004 Republican candidate for Senate from Colorado, back when that great state was still a Red State.

Their brands are some of the most iconic beer brands in the world, including Coors Light, Miller Lite, Molson Canadian, Carling, Staropramen, Coors Banquet, Blue Moon Belgian White, Blue Moon LightSky, Vizzy, Leinenkugel's Summer Shandy, Creemore Springs, Hop Valley and more.

Molson Coors Beverage Company is a publicly traded company that operates through Molson Coors North America and Molson Coors Europe, and is traded on the New York and Canadian Stock Exchange (TAP).

Company Name	Molson Coors
CEO	Gavin D. Hattersley
Twitter Handle	@MolsonCoors
Instagram Handle	@MolsonCoors
Facebook Handle	@MolsonCoors
LinkedIn Handle	/company/molson-coors/
YouTube Channel	Molson Coors
Website	**molsoncoors.com**
Stock Symbol	**TAP.A (NYSE)**
Industry	Beer Company
What Makes Them Conservative	92% of its contributions go to Republicans and Conservatives

103. Yum! Brands

Yum! Brands, Inc. (or Yum!) is an American fast food corporation listed on the Fortune 1000. Yum! operates the brands KFC, Pizza Hut, Taco Bell, and The Habit Burger Grill. Yum! previously also owned Long John Silver's and A&W Restaurants.

Based in Louisville, Kentucky, Yum! is one of the world's largest fast food restaurant companies in terms of the number of restaurants under its umbrella. In 2016, Yum! had 43,617 restaurants (including 2,859 that were company-owned and 40,758 that were franchised) in 135 nations and territories worldwide. Yum is a $6 billion a year company, and they are a mainstay of the MAGA Fund!

Company Name	Yum! Brands
CEO	David Gibbs
Twitter Handle	@yumbrands
Instagram Handle	@yum_brands
Facebook Handle	@yumbrands
LinkedIn Handle	/company/yum-brands/
YouTube Channel	Yum! Brands, Inc.
Website	**yum.com**
Stock Symbol	YUM (NYSE)
Industry	Restaurant Company
What Makes Them Conservative	87% of its contributions go to Republicans and Conservatives

104. **Tyson Foods Inc.**

Tyson Foods Inc. was established by John W. Tyson in 1935. As of 2021, it employed 137,000 people, with $47 billion in revenue. 1 in 5 pounds of beef, pork and chicken consumed in the USA is provided by Tyson Foods.

The company supplies chicken, beef and pork to retail grocers, broad line foodservice distributors and national fast food and full-service restaurant chains. It provides chicken supplies to all brand chains, including KFC and Taco Bell, as well as McDonald's, Burger King, small restaurant businesses, and prisons. It manufactures a wide variety of processed meat products at its 123 food processing plants. It produces products such as Buffalo wings, boneless Buffalo wings, chicken nuggets and tenders. It operates through four segments: Chicken, Beef, Pork and Prepared Foods. In 2019, Tyson introduced a line of plant-based products called Raised & Rooted that produces vegetarian burgers, nuggets, and sausages.

Here's an awesome quote from their website "We're passionate about food. We believe food is more than sustenance, it's a vehicle for good. As we continue to grow, we're embracing our responsibility to drive positive change, solve problems, and make the world a little better every day."

They are not perfect from a conservative point of view, they have bought into some of the ESG nonsense, but they do donate heavily to the Republican party and are a mainstay of the MAGA Fund.

Company Name	Tyson Foods Inc.
CEO	Donnie King
Twitter Handle	@TysonFoods
Instagram Handle	@TysonFoods
Facebook Handle	@TysonFoods
LinkedIn Handle	/company/tyson-foods/
YouTube Channel	Tyson Foods
Website	**tysonfoods.com**
Stock Symbol	**TSN (NYSE)**
Industry	Food Company
What Makes Them Conservative	The overwhelming majority of its contributions go to Republicans and Conservatives

105. Lowe's

Lowe's is an iconic American home improvement retailer. Headquartered in Mooresville, North Carolina, the company operates a chain of retail stores in the United States and Canada. As of February 2021, Lowe's and its related businesses operates 2,197 home improvement and hardware stores in North America.

Lowe's is the second-largest hardware chain in the United States behind rival The Home Depot. Lowe's was started by Lucius Lowe in 1921 and is a mainstay of the MAGA Fund. Nicky shop's there often, and really likes it!

Company Name	Lowe's Companies
CEO	Marvin Ellison
Twitter Handle	@Lowes
Instagram Handle	@LowesHomeImprovement
Facebook Handle	@Lowes
LinkedIn Handle	/company/ lowe's-home-improvement/
YouTube Channel	Lowes
Website	**lowes.com**
Stock Symbol	**LOW (NYSE)**
Industry	Retailer
What Makes Them Conservative	The majority of its contributions go to Republicans and Conservatives

The Patriotic
Podcasters

There are a number of patriotic podcasters that we recommend you listen to. Not all of them have political shows, and there are a couple that don't identify as conservatives, but they are all patriots who love America and freedom. They are all good capitalists, against the woke mind-virus, and ardent champions of free speech. We recommend you listen to their shows and support their companies.

106. The Joe Rogan Experience

The Joe Rogan Experience is a podcast hosted by American comedian, presenter, and UFC color commentator Joe Rogan. It launched on December 24, 2009, on YouTube. By 2015, it was one of the world's most popular podcasts, regularly receiving millions of views per episode, also including a wide array of guests, including Elon Musk, whistleblower Edward Snowden, and former Congresswoman Tulsi Gabbard. Since December 2020, the podcast has been exclusively available on Spotify, with highlights uploaded onto the main Joe Rogan Experience YouTube channel. The podcast was originally recorded in Los Angeles. Production was moved to Austin, Texas after the podcast was exclusively licensed on Spotify in 2020.

Although most episodes feature entertainers, academics, comics, UFC fighters, and other non-political figures, Rogan has taken a hard stance in favor of free speech, and has brought on figures like Alex Jones, Jordan Peterson, and Dr. Robert Malone on his show. He has hit back hard against the so-called Covid vaccine and pushed alternative therapies like monoclonal anti-bodies and Ivermectin, as well as vitamin drips as effective remedies to treat Covid. Dr. Malone and others who have been opposed to the prevailing fake Covid narrative have been given a platform and a respectful hearing by Rogan.

Joe Rogan may not be a conservative, but he is an American patriot and a man who has fearlessly stepped up and been counted when the forces of tyranny attempted to make him heel. He deserves your support.

Company Name	The Joe Rogan Experience
Host	Joe Rogan
Twitter Handle	@joerogan
Instagram Handle	@joerogan
Facebook Handle	@joerogan
LinkedIn Handle	/company/joe-rogan-328562218/
YouTube Channel	Joe Rogan
Website	**joerogan.com**
Industry	Podcasting & Media
What Makes Them Conservative	He is a huge free speech advocate

107. Valuetainment—Patrick Bet David

Nicky will admit to being biased because Patrick Bet David is a fellow Assyrian-Iranian born Christian. But Valuetainment and Patrick Bet David are American treasures. The company was founded in 2013, as a media brand with "the purpose of teaching fundamentals of entrepreneurship and personal development while inspiring people to break from limiting beliefs or other constraints." Many people have called it "the best channel for entrepreneurs" online, and it has become a powerful media network providing news, other content partners and a weekly podcast.

Patrick has a deep love of America, and he served in the US Army before beginning his entrepreneurial career. He has not come out and called himself a conservative, but he calls himself a capitalist and he will bring on guests that the Evil Left hates, such as Andrew Tate, Dennis Prager, and Jordan Peterson.

Patrick and his channel provide great content for entrepreneurs, and he is an inspirational figure that deserves our support.

Company Name	Valuetainment
Host	Patrick Bet David
Twitter Handle	@ValuetainmentTV
Instagram Handle	@Valuetainment
Facebook Handle	@ValuetainmentMedia
LinkedIn Handle	/company/ValuetainmentMedia
YouTube Channel	Valuetainment
Website	**PatrickBetDavid.com**
Industry	Podcasting & Media
What Makes Them Conservative	He is a capitalist, free speech advocate

108. The Thought Leader Revolution/Sovereign Man Podcast

The Thought Leader Revolution & The Sovereign Man (TTLR & SM) are the co-author of this book Nicky Billou's podcasts. Nicky is a committed champion of freedom, free expression and free enterprise.

The Thought Leader Revolution is his main business podcast, where he interviews some of the top business minds in the world to get them to share their tips and insights for freedom-loving entrepreneurs. His vision is to bring people the basics of successful entrepreneurship and personal & professional development, while uplifting them and encouraging them to break free from their limiting beliefs. It has been called "the best podcast for conservative and Christian entrepreneurs" online, and it has become a powerful voice for success, capitalism, and freedom, with a twice-weekly podcast. He has also interviewed some of the top freedom lovers in the world on his show, including Wayne Allyn Root, George Ross of the Apprentice, Pat King (one of the key organizers of the legendary Canadian trucker-led Freedom Convoy), and Phelim McAleer, the producer of the movie *My Son Hunter*.

The Sovereign Man is a podcast for men, one where every week, Nicky has the conversations that matter to men. The Left has created an environment in society that is actively hostile to traditional masculinity and to men. They are deliberately creating confusion amongst younger men and boys so that there are no strong men to stand up to them. This podcast is one where men and masculinity are celebrated, and men are taught about honorable masculinity, and features interviews with thought leaders in the work of men such as bestselling author and former Navy SEAL Clint Emerson, Ernest Emerson of Emerson Knives, former Marine Raider Nick Koumalatsos, and million book selling bestselling authors Lt. Colonel David Grossman and G. Michael Hopf (the man who wrote the famous poem "Hard Times Create Strong Men, Strong Men Create Good Times, Good Times Create Weak Men, Weak Men Create Hard Times"). It has been called "the best men's self-improvement podcast" online.

Nicky is also a frequent guest commentator providing expertise on matters of international politics and the global fight for freedom on shows such as Wayne Allyn Root (WAR)'s and Ezra Levant's on Rebel News.

Podcast Name	The Thought Leader Revolution
Host	Nicky Billou
Twitter Handle	@NickyBillou
Instagram Handle	@NickyBillou
Facebook Handle	@thethoughtleaderrevolution
LinkedIn Handle	/company/NickyBillou/
Rumble Channel	@PersianPoet
Website	**TheThoughtLeaderRevolution.com**
Industry	Podcasting & Media
What Makes Them Conservative	Nicky Billou's Business Podcast!!!!

Podcast Name	The Sovereign Man
Host	Nicky Billou
Twitter Handle	@NickyBillou
Instagram Handle	@sovereign_man_movement
Facebook Handle	@TheSovereignMan
LinkedIn Handle	/company/NickyBillou/
Rumble Channel	@PersianPoet
Website	**SovereignMan.ca**
Industry	Podcasting & Media
What Makes Them Conservative	Nicky Billou's Men's Podcast!!!!

109. **Jocko Podcast**

The Jocko Podcast is the podcast of American patriot, entrepreneur, bestselling author, and decorated former Navy SEAL Jocko Willink. He is most famous as the author of the bestselling book *Extreme Ownership: How U.S. Navy SEALs Lead and Win,* with Leif Babin. He and Leif co-founded Echelon Front, a leading-edge consulting company for business organizations where he is a leadership instructor, speaker, and executive coach. Echelon Front is one of the world's top leadership consultancies, and Nicky is a grateful follower of Jocko and his work. His clients include individuals, teams, companies, and organizations across a wide range of industries and fields.

Jocko earned his patriotism the old-fashioned way, by spending 20 years in the U.S. Navy SEAL Teams, starting in the enlisted ranks and rising to become a SEAL commissioned officer. As the commander of SEAL Team Three's Task Unit Bruiser during the battle of Ramadi, he orchestrated SEAL operations that helped the "Ready First" Brigade of the US Army's First Armored Division bring stability to that ultra-violent, war-torn city. Task Unit Bruiser became the most highly decorated Special Operations Unit of the Iraq War. His experience there was the basis for Extreme Ownership and reflected new and original thinking on the subjects of leadership and winning.

Jocko returned from Iraq to serve as Officer-in-Charge of training for all West Coast SEAL Teams. There, he spearheaded the development of leadership training and personally instructed and mentored the next generation of SEAL leaders who have continued to perform with great success on the battlefield.

This role prepared him to launch Echelon Front and his podcast after he retired from the Navy in 2010. Both teach the hard-won leadership principles of the battlefield to help others lead and win.

Jocko is a true American original, and a man worthy of your support. Listen to his podcast and buy his books and services.

Podcast Name	Jocko Podcast
Host	Jocko Willink
Twitter Handle	@JockoWillink
Instagram Handle	@JockoWillink
Facebook Handle	@JkoWillink
LinkedIn Handle	/company/JockFuel
YouTube Channel	@JockoPodcastOfficial
Website	**JockoPodcast.com**
Industry	Podcasting & Media
What Makes Them Conservative	Patriot, a man who has actually fought & bled for America as a Navy SEAL

110. The Dan Bongino Show

Dan Bongino is a deeply conservative radio show host, podcast host, frequent television political commentator, and New York Times best-selling author whose books include *Life Inside the Bubble*, about his career as a Secret Service agent, *The Fight: A Secret Service Agent's Inside Account of Security Failings and the Political Machine*, and *Spygate: The Attempted Sabotage of Donald J. Trump*. Bongino was formerly a Secret Service agent from 2006 to 2011, serving in the Obama and Bush administrations.

He served as a New York City Police Department (NYPD) officer from 1995 to 1999. He is also a commentator on international security and political strategy for outlets such as FOX News and others.

Dan is a genuine American patriot, and someone with a massive following who is willing to tell the truth. He deserves your support! Buy his books and listen to and watch his shows!

Podcast Name	The Dan Bongino Show
Host	Dan Bongino
Twitter Handle	@DBongino
Instagram Handle	@DBongino
Facebook Handle	@Dan.Bongino
LinkedIn Handle	N/A
Rumble Channel	@Bongino
Website	**bongino.com**
Industry	Podcasting & Media
What Makes Them Conservative	Dan is a huge supporter of President Trump and of Freedom!

111. Bill O'Reilly's No Spin News

Bill O'Reilly is an American conservative commentator, journalist, author, and television host. He began his broadcasting career during the late 1970s as a reporter for local television stations in the United States. He later joined CBS News and ABC News as a national reporter. He anchored the hugely popular tabloid television program *Inside Edition* from 1989 to 1995. Bill joined the Fox News Channel in 1996 and hosted *The O'Reilly Factor* until 2017. It was at Fox that Bill became a megastar, with *The O'Reilly Factor* becoming the highest-rated cable news show for 16 years. He is the biggest selling non-fiction author of the past 15+ years with his *Killing* book series, co-authored with Martin Dugard.

In 2017, he left Fox and launched his own podcast, *The No Spin News*. It is one of the biggest and most popular podcasts in the USA. Bill is a genuine patriot. He is someone who fearlessly pursues the truth, and his show is full of great insights and amazing guests. He deserves your support, so please subscribe to his podcast and buy his books!

Podcast Name	The No Spin News
Host	Bill O'Reilly
Twitter Handle	@BillOReilly
Instagram Handle	@BillOReilly
Facebook Handle	@BillOReillyOfficial
LinkedIn Handle	/company/billoreilly-com/
YouTube Channel	Bill O'Reilly
Website	**billoreilly.com**
Industry	Podcasting & Media
What Makes Them Conservative	Bill is an unabashed American patriot and unafraid to say so on his show daily.

112. The Mark Levin Show

The Mark Levin Show is one of the most popular radio shows and podcasts in the conservative media space. Mark is a stalwart conservative who has been a valiant champion of freedom. Mark is an American lawyer, author, and radio personality. He hosts the syndicated radio show *The Mark Levin Show*, as well as *Life, Liberty & Levin* on Fox News. Levin worked in the administration of the Great President Ronald Reagan and was a chief of staff for Reagan's legendary Attorney General Edwin Meese. He is the bestselling author of 7 books, and one of the sharpest legal minds in the country.

Since 2015, Mark Levin has been editor-in-chief of the *Conservative Review* and is known for his no-holds barred commentary excoriating the Left and the Marxists in the Democrat Party. He is a staunch supporter of President Trump and a man who derives your time, attention, and support!

Podcast Name	The Mark Levin Show
Host	Mark Levin
Twitter Handle	@MarkLevinShow
Instagram Handle	@MarkLevinShow
Facebook Handle	@MarkLevinShow
LinkedIn Handle	in/mark-levin-a1096b253/
Rumble Channel	@MarkLevinShow
Website	**marklevinshow.com**
Industry	Podcasting & Media
What Makes Them Conservative	Mark is a huge supporter of President Trump and foe to the Left!

113. Bannon's War Room

Steve Bannon's War Room is one of the Top 5 conservative podcasts in America today. Bannon helped co-found Breitbart News with the late, great Andrew Breitbart. He is a former Naval Officer, investment banker with Goldman Sachs, and a producer in Hollywood. He was part of the brain trust that helped President Trump in his 2016 campaign to win the White House and served as an advisor to the President for 8 months.

The Left hates Bannon and has organized a lawfare campaign to unjustly send him to prison. That has not stopped Steve from fearlessly exposing the Left and promoting MAGA and MAGA candidates. Steve Bannon is a genuine American patriot, and he deserves your support as he fights the good fight for America's future!

Podcast Name	Steve Bannon's War Room
Host	Steve Bannon
Twitter Handle	@Bannons_WarRoom
Instagram Handle	N/A
Facebook Handle	N/A
LinkedIn Handle	N/A
Rumble Channel	@BannonsWarRoom
Website	**warroom.org**
Industry	Podcasting & Media
What Makes Them Conservative	Steve is the original thinker behind the intellectual framework of MAGA!

114. Glenn Beck—The Blaze

Glenn Beck is an American original. He is a conservative political commentator, radio host, entrepreneur, and television producer. He is the CEO, founder, and owner of Mercury Radio Arts, the parent company of his popular television and radio network, The Blaze. He hosts the *Glenn Beck Radio Program*, a talk-radio show nationally syndicated on Premiere Radio Networks. He also hosts the Glenn Beck television program, which airs on The Blaze. He has written six awesome New York Times–bestselling books.

Glenn launched The Blaze in 2011 after leaving Fox News. He hosts an hour-long afternoon program, The Glenn Beck Program, on weekdays, and a three-hour morning radio show; both are broadcast on The Blaze. Beck is also the producer of The Blaze's *For the Record*.

Beck is a staunch defender of traditional American values. He started off as a "Never Trumper", but was man enough to admit that he was wrong about Trump, and became one of his most enthusiastic supporters. He and The Blaze deserve your support, and you should buy and read his books!

Podcast Name	The Glenn Beck Podcast
Host	Glenn Beck
Twitter Handle	@glennbeck
Instagram Handle	@glennbeck
Facebook Handle	@glennbeck
LinkedIn Handle	/company/the-blaze/
Rumble Channel	@glennbeck
Website	**glennbeck.com**
Industry	Podcasting & Media
What Makes Them Conservative	Glenn is a longtime champion of freedom and conservative media figure

115. Clay Travis—Outkick & The Clay Travis & Buck Sexton Show

Clay Travis is one of the very few sports commentators who has not succumbed to the woke virus that has infected American sports media. He became famous when he was on a CNN show and boldly proclaimed that he only believes in two things, boobs and the First Amendment. The host of the show, Brooke Baldwin, freaked out at him, as did the other virtue-signaling guest. She attempted to shame him into walking back his comments, but he refused. That clip went viral, and a new media star was born.

Clay built his own sports media empire, OutKick, initially with Jason Whitlock. He ended up selling it to Fox for a rumored 9 figures. After the death of the great Rush Limbaugh, he and Buck Sexton were asked to do a show filling-in Rush's old radio time slot. Clay is one of the most fearless and popular radio and podcast hosts in America, and he deserves your attention and support! Buy his books and listen to his programs!

Podcast Name	OutKick/ Clay Travis & Buck Sexton Show
Host	Clay Travis
Twitter Handle	@ClayTravis
Instagram Handle	@ClayTravisOutKick
Facebook Handle	@ClayTravis
LinkedIn Handle	/company/outkick/
YouTube Channel	OutKick
Website	**OutKick.com**
Industry	Podcasting & Media
What Makes Them Conservative	Clay is a fearless champion of freedom and a foe of cancel culture and the Left

116. Steven Crowder—Louder With Crowder

Steven Crowder is a Canadian-born political commentator with a massive following on YouTube. He began his career at the age of 12 as a voiceover artist, moving on to being a standup comic by 17. He started uploading satirical conservative political videos on YouTube in 2009, and his channel has nearly 6 million subscribers. Due to YouTube's pro-censorship policies, he also began a Rumble Channel in 2021, which is becoming increasingly popular.

Crowder is a fierce defender of free speech, and mercilessly mocks the Left for its appalling hypocrisy and assaults on freedom, including the Covid hypocrisy over vaccines and lockdowns. He has a subscription service called Mug Club, and his daily YouTube/Rumble Show is hilarious. We highly recommend your watch it and support the amazing Steven Crowder!

Podcast Name	Louder With Crowder
Host	Steven Crowder
Twitter Handle	@scrowder
Instagram Handle	@LouderWithCrowder
Truth Social Handle	@StevenCrowder
Rumble Channel	Steven Crowder
YouTube Channel	Steven Crowder
Website	**mugclubforever.com**
Industry	Podcasting & Media
What Makes Them Conservative	Steven is one of the funniest comedians alive and a committed champion of freedom in the age of the Branch Covidians.

117. Matt Walsh

Matthew Walsh is a proudly conservative political commentator and author, one who particularly infuriates and stupefies the nutty Left. Matt hosts *The Matt Walsh Show* podcast and is a regular columnist for The Daily Wire. He has authored four books and starred in The Daily Wire online hit documentary film *What Is A Woman?*

Matt is a former talk radio host for stations in Delaware and Kentucky. He has been one of the stalwart and outspoken leaders in the battle against the transgender ideology and has campaigned against hospitals providing so-called gender affirming surgery for confused children, many of whom have ended up regretting being pressured and brainwashed into making this so-called choice at a point in their lives when they aren't mature or ready enough to make such a drastic change that cannot so easily be undone. For this alone, Matt deserves your support. Please listen to his programs, watch his documentaries, and buy his books!

Podcast Name	The Matt Walsh Show
Host	Matt Walsh
Twitter Handle	@MattWalshBlog
Instagram Handle	@MattWalshBlog
Facebook Handle	@MattWalsh
Rumble Channel	Matt Walsh
YouTube Channel	Matt Walsh
Website	**MattWalshBlog.com**
Industry	Podcasting & Media
What Makes Them Conservative	Matt is a fearless champion of freedom and defender of women and children against the transgender cult

118. Ben Shapiro—The Ben Shapiro Show

Ben Shapiro is the co-founder of The Daily Wire and hosts a daily political podcast and live radio show called *The Ben Shapiro Show*. He has been a fearless conservative speaker on many college campuses, taking on leftists and leftist nonsense, and is the author of 11 bestselling books. Ben is one of the smartest people in media today, and he is a deep thinker on many of the issues that matter to conservative Americans. The Daily Wire, under his leadership, has become an emerging media empire and is making traditionally-themed movies to compete with woke Hollywood.

Ben is also an attorney and columnist. At the tender age of 17, he became the youngest nationally syndicated columnist in the United States. He writes columns for Creators Syndicate, Newsweek, and Ami Magazine, and is the editor emeritus for The Daily Wire. He was editor-at-large of Breitbart News between 2012 and 2016. Ben is a champion for freedom and traditional American values, and he deserves your support! Listen to his program, buy his books, and support The Daily Wire!

Podcast Name	The Ben Shapiro Show
Host	Ben Shapiro
Twitter Handle	@BenShapiro
Instagram Handle	@OfficialBenShapiro
Facebook Handle	@BenShapiro
Rumble Channel	Ben Shapiro
YouTube Channel	Ben Shapiro
Website	**dailywire.com/author/ben-shapiro**
Industry	Podcasting & Media
What Makes Them Conservative	Ben founded The Daily Wire, and has been fighting the good fight against the Left on campuses for over 20 years

119. Candace Owens

Candace Owens is one of the leading conservative voices in the modern era. Her first political YouTube video was released in 2017, and it resulted in her meteoric rise to the top of the conservative media universe. She is the host of *Candace*, a political talk show on The Daily Wire network. She is known for her anti-lockdown and anti-Covid vaccine views, and she has a massive following on social media. She is the best-selling author of the *Blackout: How Black America Can Make Its Second Escape From The Democrat Plantation*, and the producer of the documentary *The Greatest Lie Ever Sold*, which is an exposé on the fraudulent BLM movement. From 2017 to 2019, she was the Director of Communications at Turning Point USA, and since 2022, she has been one of the stars of The Daily Wire network.

Candace is married to George Farmer, the CEO of Parler, one of the other companies on this list. She is a committed champion of freedom and was one of the earliest and most vociferous voices against lockdowns and BLM. She deserves your support. Listen to her program and buy her book!

Podcast Name	Candace
Host	Candace Owens
Twitter Handle	@RealCandace
Instagram Handle	@RealCandaceOwens
Facebook Handle	@CandaceOwens
Parler Handle	@Candace
YouTube Channel	RealCandaceO
Website	**candaceowens.com**
Industry	Podcasting & Media
What Makes Them Conservative	Candace has fought the good fight against the Left on campuses and on costal media since 2017, and been very effective doing it

120. Dave Rubin—The Rubin Report

Dave Rubin is a conservative commentator with a popular YouTube channel and podcast, *The Rubin Report*, which also airs on Blaze TV. The channel has had over 500 million views on YouTube. Dave is a former liberal whose show was initially part of leftist Cenk Uygur's Young Turks platform. However, he left the show when Uygur lied and attacked Bill Maher and Sam Harris over their tense exchange with leftist actor Ben Affleck about the relationship between terrorism and Islamic doctrine.

On October 23, 2014, Sam Harris sat down for a three hour debate with Cenk Uygur, the founder of The Young Turks. Rubin states that this exchange helped open his eyes to the lying ways of the Left. "The way he (Uygur) became the leader of the group just relentlessly lying about Sam, and then to sit there for three hours with the guy and just double down on every lie—it showed such a character flaw." It also appalled him to witness Cenk Uygur's vicious and vile attacks on Fox News commentator David Webb, and the political Left's wicked response to the Charlie Hebdo shooting.

Dave is a gay conservative, and a friend of President Trump's. He has moved his show from LA to the Free State of Florida. He has written 2 bestselling books. He deserves your support, so buy his books and listen to his show!

Podcast Name	The Rubin Report
Host	Dave Rubin
Twitter Handle	@RubinReport
Instagram Handle	@RubinReport
Facebook Handle	@RubinReport
Rumble Channel	Rubin Report
YouTube Channel	Rubin Report
Website	**rubinreport.tv**
Industry	Podcasting & Media
What Makes Them Conservative	Dave Rubin bravely left the Left, and has been a stalwart champion for America and a fearless foe of wokism

121. Charlie Kirk—Turning Point USA & The Charlie Kirk Show

Charlie Kirk is the Founder and President of Turning Point USA, the most important national student movement dedicated to identifying, organizing, and empowering young people to promote the principles of traditional America, free markets and limited government, and combat the evils of leftism, wokism, and crypto-fascism.

Here is an excellent excerpt from the TPUSA website

"With representation on over 2,000 high school and college campuses nationwide and over 160 full-time staff, Turning Point USA is the largest and fastest-growing conservative youth activist organization in the country. At just 28-years-old, Charlie has appeared on CNBC, Fox News, and FOX Business News over 600 times, is a columnist at Newsweek and The Hill and was named to the Forbes "30 under 30" list. Charlie was also the youngest speaker at the 2016 Republican National Convention and is the author of two books, and his most recent title, *The MAGA Doctrine: The Only Ideas That Will Win The Future* is a #1 Best Seller. Charlie is also the Chairman of Students for Trump, which activated over one million new college voters on campuses in battleground states in the lead up to the 2020 presidential election."

"In 2019, Charlie was granted an honorary doctorate from Liberty University, citing his exceptional leadership and energetic voice for conservatives. His social media reaches over 100 million people per month and according to Axios, he is one of the "top 10 most engaged" Twitter handles in the world, behind only President Trump among conservatives. Charlie is the host of *"The Charlie Kirk Show*—which regularly ranks among the top 15 news shows on Apple podcast charts—where Charlie delivers in-depth analysis of the modern political and cultural landscape, mixing in philosophy and history with his signature campus activism, along with interviews of some of the most influential people of our time."

Charlie and his organization deserve your support. You should donate money to them, buy his books, and listen to his awesome podcast.

Podcast Name	The Charlie Kirk Show
Host	Charlie Kirk
Twitter Handle	@CharlieKirk11
Instagram Handle	@CharlieKirk1776
Facebook Handle	@RealCharlieKirk
Rumble Channel	Turning Point USA
YouTube Channel	Real Charlie Kirk
Website	**charliekirk.com**
Industry	Podcasting & Media & Activism
What Makes Them Conservative	Charlie runs the most important conservative student organization in America. He is an activist who is working hard to win young hearts and minds for conservatism

122. Greg Gutfeld—Gutfeld!, The Five, The One With Greg Gutfeld

Greg Gutfeld is a libertarian political satirist and humorist. He is the former editor of the magazine *Men's Health*. But he is best known as the co-host of the iconic daily hit show *The Five* and as the former host of the legendary Fox News Channel programs *The Greg Gutfeld Show* and *Red Eye* where he covered a variety of topics, including news, entertainment, sports, and gossip, mercilessly skewering the Evil Left at every opportunity.

He is now the host of the most watched Late Night TV show in America, *GUTFELD!* on the Fox News Channel, where he parodies leftists, Marxists, current events and converses on key issues with his trademark awesome humor.

The turncoats at The Bulwark call him "the most dangerous man on television." According to them, unlike other media darlings, "Gutfeld's stuff actually is subversive, a stink bomb hurled into every faculty lounge, mainstream newsroom, movie studio, and nonprofit boardroom in America."

He's been published in countless magazines. In his free time, Greg writes for his own community website, *The Gutter* where he covers every lifestyle topic imaginable with his unique comedic conservative-libertarian perspective.

He is the author of nine books, among them, five New York Times Best Sellers, *The Joy of Hate, Not Cool, How to be Right, The Gutfeld Monologues* and his most recent *The Plus: Self-Help for People Who Hate Self-Help*.

Greg is awesome, and he deserves your support! Watch his show, listen to his podcast, buy his books, attend his live comedy events, and introduce his work to your liberal family members and friends!

Podcast Name	**GUTFELD!**
Host	Greg Gutfeld
Twitter Handle	@GregGutfeld
Instagram Handle	@RealGregGutfeld
Facebook Handle	@GGutfeld
Rumble Channel	N/A
YouTube Channel	Fox News
Website	**ggutfeld.com**
Industry	Podcasting & Media
What Makes Them Conservative	Greg is the funniest comedian on TV, and he turns his incredible wit on mocking the Left and upholding freedom every day.

123. Triggered—Donald Trump, Jr.

No list of Patriotic Podcasters would be complete without the addition of the great Donald Trump, Jr.

He just signed a multiyear, multimillion dollar exclusive deal with Rumble, another mainstay of this book, to air his show twice a week. The name of his show is *Triggered*, and it is a powerful salvo against the censorious Big Tech leftists who are trying to silence conservatives and conservatism.

It provides a space where conservatives can take the fight to the evil Left in the culture war. This show will help Rumble gain more users, and help it become the dominant video sharing platform in the world

Trump Jr. is among the vanguard of the growth of Rumble, and he and other high profile users like Andrew Tate have helped cause a decline in followership for Woke Tech and Woke Entertainment.

On his first episode, he said "I think for the first time in recent history, we are actually winning," citing the recent struggles of Disney and Netflix as examples of the public rejecting woke corporations and their horrible virtue signaling.

In a recent interview with Breitbart News, Don Jr. explained how his podcast's presence on Rumble would give momentum to the "parallel economy" of platforms and companies that celebrate conservative voices. "A big focus of what I've been doing sort of outside of my daily duties is finding those same companies who are starting in front of the parallel economy where conservatives are saying, 'well, you're there, you're canceling my insurance, or you're canceling my banking or you're canceling my phones, or whatever it may be, because I'm a conservative."

Don Jr. deserves your support! Listen to him and his show, and help him defeat wokism and build up the parallel economy.

Podcast Name	Triggered
Host	Donald Trump Jr.
Twitter Handle	@DonaldJTrumpJr
Instagram Handle	@DonaldJTrumpJr
Facebook Handle	@DonaldJTrumpJr
Rumble Channel	Donald J Trump Jr.
YouTube Channel	N/A
Website	**trump.com**
Industry	Podcasting & Media
What Makes Them Conservative	Don Jr. is a committed and fearless champion for freedom and takes on the Left and stands up for America

"Never, ever, ever, ever, ever give up."

Winston Churchill

CONCLUSION

We are both very hopeful that the tide against wokism and liberalism is turning. Governor DeSantis's strong stand against Disney, and its own obsession with sexualized content for children resulted in its streaming channel Disney+ losing $1.5 billion, and its latest movie, **Strange World**, which features openly gay characters and sexual themes for kids under the age of 8 tanking, earning just $24 million, versus a production budget of $180 million. Disney fired clueless CEO Bob Chapek and brought back former CEO Bob Iger. While Iger has also made noises supporting trans ideology, he has woken up to reality and backed away from picking political fights with the state of Florida and is making noises about staying out of politics and making quality family entertainment. The jury is still out—"Trust but verify" as our hero Ronald Reagan once said.

This is but one partial win in the battle against the woke infestation of American corporations, and while it is an important one, we have a long way to go.

We need tough political leaders like DeSantis to stand up to the woke bullies, and to strike back. DeSantis just stood up to Apple, and demanded Congress investigate it for abuse of monopolistic power, if it removed the newly non-woke Twitter from its App Store. Apple very quickly assured Elon Musk that it had no intention of removing Twitter from the App Store.

That's a second skirmish win (for the moment).

But the war is not over. We need to keep pushing against the woke companies and to keep buying from the non-woke companies. Now that we have Twitter on the side of the angels (or so it seems), let's use Twitter to both promote both our boycott and BUYcott lists, so that we can help you, as a patriotic and conservative American consumer, avoid supporting brands that hate you and your values, and support the brands that love you and share your values.

Take a good look at all the companies in this book. If you can buy from them, please do so. Encourage your friends to do so. Encourage your family members to do so. There is no reason whatsoever for you to give your money to companies that hate America, or who are too scared to stand up to the woke bullies. There is every reason for you to give your money to companies that love America and are proud to stand up for her and what she stands for.

You need to buy groceries. Buy from Publix. You need to buy beer. Buy Bud and Yeungling. You need to buy wine. Buy We The People wine. You need a new knife. Buy an Emerson. You need to unwind and watch a sports game. Watch a UFC event. You need some ice cream. Buy from Blue Bell Creameries. You need sheets and bedding and slippers. Buy from MyPillow and support a great American, Mike Lindell. Do you need household goods? Buy from <u>GreatPatriotStore.com</u>. You need a hotel- stay at Marriott, Omni, or a Trump Hotel. If you want to spend a weekend in Vegas—stay at The Venetian, or Red Rock Resort (Station Casinos).

Buying from companies on this list will make you proud of being an American, and proud to be sending your dollars to good old fashioned American companies.

To quote from a great song, *American Made*, sung by an American band, The Oak Ridge Boys,

> *Seems everything I buy these days*
> *Has got a foreign name.*
> *From the kind of car I drive*
> *To my video game.*
> *I got a NIKON camera*
> *A Sony color TV*
> *But the one that I love is from the U.S.A.*
> *And standing next to me.*
>
> *My baby is American Made*
> *Born and bred in the U.S.A.*

From her silky long hair to her sexy long legs
My baby is American Made.

She looks good in her tight blue jeans
She bought in Mexico.
And she loves wearing French perfume
Everywhere we go
But when it comes to the loving part
One thing is true
My baby's genuine U.S.A.
Red, white and blue.

My baby is American Made
Born and bred in the U.S.A.
From her silky long hair to her sexy long legs
My baby is American Made.

My baby is American Made,
Born and bred in the U.S.A.
From her silky long hair to her sexy long legs
My baby is American Made.

My baby is American Made, o yes she is.
Born and bred in the U.S.A.
From her silky long hair to her sexy long legs
My baby is American Made.

My baby is American Made, ah hum.
Born and bred in the U.S.A.
From her silky long hair to her sexy long legs
My baby is American Made.

God bless you, God Bless America, and God bless all American patriots.

Wayne & Nicky
January 31, 2023

ABOUT THE AUTHORS

Wayne Allyn Root (aka WAR) is not your typical CEO. He prefers the titles SOB, HEB and MR—for "Son of a Butcher" "Human Energizer Bunny" and "Mr. Relentless." The media calls him "the conservative warrior" and "the capitalist evangelist."

2022 was quite the year of a lifetime for Wayne! He was Knighted "Sir Wayne Allyn Root." Wayne was inducted into the Nevada Broadcasters Hall of Fame. And he fulfilled a lifetime goal of being included in "SWANK: the 14th Annual International Best Dressed List."

Even more impressive, Wayne became the host of two new television shows in late 2022. "America's Top Ten Countdown with Wayne Allyn Root" on Real America's Voice TV Network on Saturdays at Noon ET…and "Wayne Allyn Root: Raw & Unfiltered" streamed daily on Lindell TV (at FrankSpeech.com). It airs Monday-Friday at 7 PM ET on Lindell TV 2.

Wayne is the bestselling author of 15 books- including *The Great Patriot Protest & Boycott Book (with Nicky Billou)*, *TRUMP RULES*, *The Power of Relentless*, *The Ultimate Obama Survival Guide* and *The Murder of the Middle Class.*

President Trump has said of Wayne (in national TV interviews), "Wayne knows how to win"…"Wayne always gets good ratings"…"Wayne has courage"…and "It's always great being with Wayne. We've done some great work together."

Premier Radio Network host Bill Cunningham calls Wayne "the most fearless conservative in America." Former Presidential advisor and TV host Steve Bannon calls Wayne "the great one" and "the OG (Original Gangster) and the ether of the MAGA and Trump movement."

Wayne is a high-energy, dynamic, outspoken, fiery, combative, controversial, unapologetic, in-your-face, New York businessman, Las Vegas gaming CEO, reality TV show producer, and former Presidential candidate, turned conservative media superstar.

Remind you of anyone?

That could be why even the liberal, woke, Daily Beast said of Wayne, "Root is the Las Vegas version of Trump."

Wayne is best known for his relentless energy, enthusiasm and passion for America, American exceptionalism, the great American middle class, conservatism, capitalism, economic freedom, small business, and the American Dream.

This former 2008 Libertarian Vice Presidential nominee is the host of the nationally syndicated *Wayne Allyn Root: Raw & Unscripted* on USA Radio Network daily from 6 PM to 9 PM ET.

Wayne was named to the "Talkers Heavy Hundred" list of the top 100 radio talk show hosts in America in 2019, 2020, 2021, and 2022. Wayne joins the list with the superstars of talk radio, including the late Rush Limbaugh, Sean Hannity, Dave Ramsey, Mark Levin, Michael Savage, Dan Bongino, Charley Kirk, Ben Shapiro, Clay Travis and Glenn Beck.

Wayne's popular daily podcast is titled, *WAR RAW*.

Wayne's newspaper column is read in newspapers across the USA, syndicated by Creators Syndicate.

Wayne is a former lead anchorman and host of five shows at CNBC (then known as Financial News Network).

Wayne was the opening speaker at every presidential campaign event in Las Vegas for candidate Donald J. Trump. He was personally chosen by President Donald J. Trump as the opening speaker for Trump's first Las Vegas visit as President of the United States in September 2018.

Wayne speaks to conservative and business groups and conferences across the USA on the topics of conservative politics, capitalism, economics, business leadership, entrepreneurship; and of course, the "TRUMP RULES" of winning at business, politics and life.

Wayne is a S.O.B. (son of a butcher). Wayne was born into a blue-collar Jewish family. Wayne took Jesus Christ as his savior 33 years ago. This unique religious and spiritual combination of Judaism and Christianity, and Wayne's love of Israel, led Wayne to call President Trump "the greatest President in world history for the Jewish people and Israel" on national TV—leading to a liberal media meltdown across the globe. President Trump personally tweeted his thanks to Wayne multiple times.

Wayne was honored in 2006 with a 180-pound granite star on the "Las Vegas Walk of Stars." His star sits on Las Vegas Blvd in front of the Paris Resort & Casino. Wayne joins the legends of Vegas including Elvis, Liberace, Wayne Newton, Frank Sinatra, Dean Martin, Sammy Davis Jr., Bobby Darin and Siegfried & Roy.

Wayne resides in Las Vegas, Nevada with his wife Cindy and his four children.

Nicky Billou *(aka Nicky Bee)* is an immigrant from the Middle East turned into a CEO, successful entrepreneur, patriot, freedom-fighter, bestselling author, and host of the #1 podcast in the world on thought leadership, *The Thought Leader Revolution*, as well as the brand-new podcast for men called *The Sovereign Man*. Nicky is a champion for Freedom, Free Expression, and Free Enterprise. He is a passionate, enthusiastic and no-b.s. champion of America, the West, and the values that have made it a beacon for oppressed people everywhere.

He is the #1 International Best Selling Author of 8 books, including: *The Great Patriot Protest & Boycott Book: The Priceless List For Conservatives, Christians, Patriots, & 80 Million+ Trump Warriors To Cancel "cancel culture" & Save America (with Wayne Allyn Root), Finish Line Thinking™: How to Think and Win Like a Champion, The Thought Leader's Journey: A Fable of Life, The Power Of Connecting: How To Activate Profitable Relationships By Serving Your Network (with Kai Bjorn), and How To Create A Million Dollar A Year Income: The Priceless Guide For Insurance Agents, Professional Sale People, And Anyone With A Big Dream (with Perry Wong)*.

He is an in-demand and highly inspirational speaker to corporate audiences. He is an advisor and confidante to some of the most successful and dynamic entrepreneurs in Canada. He is the co-founder of eCircle Academy (www.eCircleAcademy.com) where he runs a year-long Mastermind & Educational program working with Coaches, Consultants, Corporate Trainers, Clinic Owners, Realtors, Mortgage Brokers, and other service-based Entrepreneurs, positioning them as authorities in their niche. He is the creator of the Thought Leader/Heart Leader™ Designation. He is known as The Millionaire Maker, for having helped 80+ people add 6 to 8 figures to their businesses.

He also writes on issues of business, culture, and politics for www.politicrossing.com, including interviews with Wayne Allyn Root, Amanda Milius, the producer of the movie *The Plot Against the President*, Phelim McAleer, the producer of the movie *My Son Hunter* and many others. He has also interviewed over 400 of the world's smartest and best-known thought leaders, including astronaut and #1 best-selling author Chris Hadfield; George Ross, Donald Trump's right-hand man on the Hit TV Series *The Apprentice*; Barbara Corcoran from the hit TV series *Shark Tank*, Supermodel & Business Mogul Kathy Ireland, John Maxwell the World's #1 Leadership Author, NYT #1 Bestselling Author Seth Godin, Marie Forleo, Oprah's Coach, Jack Canfield & Mark Victor Hansen: Authors Of **Chicken Soup For The Soul**, and Scott Adams, Creator of Dilbert and the bestselling author of **Winning Bigly: Persuasion In A World Where Facts Don't Matter**.

Nicky is an unapologetic champion of freedom, free expression, and free enterprise. He is a man with boundless energy and passion for winning and success and is the most American Canadian you are ever going to meet. He loves America, American exceptionalism, and believes like Lincoln that America is "the last, best hope for mankind."

"When we lost our freedom in Iran, my family and I had somewhere to go to. If we lose our freedom in America, there is nowhere we can go to. This is it. We must make our stand here and keep freedom alive."

Nicky is based in Toronto, Canada, where he resides with his 2 sons. His newest website is www.sovereignman.ca.

TO CONTACT WAYNE

Wayne Allyn Root speaks all over the USA on the topics of business, sales, leadership, and of course conservative politics. Wayne speaks to business groups, conferences and conventions. As well as GOP groups, conservative groups, and college conservative groups.

To contact Wayne for a speech or media appearance:

Wayne Allyn Root
ROOTforAmerica.com
WayneRoot@gmail.com
wayne@WayneRoot.com

PH:
(888) 444-ROOT(7668)

Address:
Silver State Radio LLC
Wayne Allyn Root
1930 Village Center Circle
Ste 3-376
Las Vegas, NV 89134

Twitter:
@RealWayneRoot

TruthSocial:
@RealWayneRoot

GETTR:
@RealWayneRoot

Parler:
@RealWayneRoot

TO CONTACT NICKY

Nicky Billou speaks all over Canada & the USA on the topics of business, sales, men's issues, thought leadership, and of course, conservative politics. Nicky speaks to business groups, conferences and conventions.

To contact Nicky Billou for a speech or media appearance:

Nicky Billou
ecircleacademy.com
nicky360.com
sovereignman.ca
TheThoughtLeaderRevolution.com
nicky@ecircle.ca

PH:
416-629-7481

Twitter:
@NickyBillou

GETTR:
@NickyBillou

Facebook:
@NickyBillou

Instagram:
@NickyBillou

Address:
25 Mallard Road
Toronto, Ontario
Canada
M3B 1S4